BURMA

★

SUPERSTAR

Addictive Recipes from the Crossroads of Southeast Asia

Desmond Tan AND **Kate Leahy**

Photography by John Lee

TEN SPEED PRESS
California | New York

For most Americans, Burma is either
an exotic place full of gold pagodas
and smiling Buddhist monks—or a country
that puts activists in jail.

PREFACE

For me, though, Burma was never either extreme. I was born in Yangon in the days when it was still called Rangoon. We lived on Tharaphi Street in a middle-class neighborhood west of downtown filled with leafy trees and low-rise apartment buildings. My dad ran a taxi service during a time when cars—mostly all beat-up sedans—were pretty rare in the city. My friends and I used this to our advantage. Without traffic, we turned Tharaphi Street into a soccer field, using rocks or whatever else we could find as goalposts.

We were a family of athletes. One of my uncles was on the national basketball team and another played for the national soccer team. Then and now, soccer is hugely important for Burmese people (*chinlone*, an old Burmese sport that resembles an elaborate game of hacky sack, may have been a precursor to modern-day soccer). In the 1960s and early 1970s, Burma's soccer team won the Southeast Asian Games five times. I thought about soccer as soon as I woke up in the morning and would play it before school, as soon as school let out, and after dinner. I joke to kids these days that because we didn't have distractions like TV or cell phones, we could turn anything into a game. We even found ways to entertain ourselves with a couple of rubber bands. (Kids these days just think I'm old.) We also found ways to get into mild forms of trouble. When neighbors put bags around guavas to protect the ripening fruit from the birds, we took it as a sign that the guavas were gift-wrapped for us, and we would steal them after dark.

While I was content with soccer and fruit stealing, my parents wanted more for me and my two brothers and sister. My family is mostly ethnically Chinese, and in the 1960s, anti-Chinese demonstrations swept through Rangoon, and tensions grew between Chinese living in Burma and the ruling Bamar ethnic group. Being Chinese meant that we were not allowed to be full Burmese citizens. In addition, by the 1970s, the economy was stagnant, with no sign of improvement on the horizon. All of this made it hard for my parents to envision a prosperous future for their kids. My mom's sister had already left the country for San Francisco. My parents decided they wanted to join her.

After years of waiting, my parents got visas for our family. We packed what we could but left most of our belongings behind. In those days, once you left, you were gone for good—no letters, no phone calls. In 1970s Burma, phones were useless anyway. Even if you had one, the chances that the person you'd want to call also had one were slim. When we drove away from Tharaphi Street, I knew I would never see my friends or uncles, aunts, or cousins again. We arrived in San Francisco's Inner Richmond neighborhood in November 1977, with $200 and whatever we could fit in our suitcases. I was eleven years old, and we were starting over.

At school, American-born Asian kids kept their distance from us newly arrived Asian kids, who dressed funny and had weird accents. It was not cool to be from Southeast Asia, and no one knew where Burma was, anyway. (This became even more confusing when the military government changed the country's name from Burma to Myanmar in 1989.) But my brothers and I were tough, and we established early on that we weren't going to be bullied. Eventually we learned how to fit in. I continued to play soccer—I still do. My parents also adapted, with my dad managing several gas stations in the city. Today, even though the Inner Richmond is notorious for its summer fog, my mom declares that she has always preferred it to Yangon's heat. Meanwhile, my siblings and I all took advantage of the sacrifices my parents had made to come to the United States. In the 1990s, I became involved in San Francisco's first tech boom, running a tech consulting firm and getting involved in real estate, which has long been a passion of mine. But although we put down new roots in San Francisco, our family kept Burmese traditions alive at home, especially in the kitchen. Even today, when I smell onion, garlic, shrimp paste, tomatoes, and chiles gently cooking, I'm transported back to Tharaphi Street.

I never learned how to cook. In Burma, it was always the girls who helped their moms in the kitchen. Boys just learned how to be good eaters. As a result, Burmese women grow up knowing how to prepare an entire repertoire of dishes from memory. Even when I left home, I lived close to my parents. With my mom nearby to cook for me, I was spoiled. My mom used to say—it was a joke but not a joke—what will you do when I die? What will you eat? I needed to find a way to assure her that I wouldn't go hungry.

I was in my twenties when my family discovered Burma Superstar, a hole-in-the-wall restaurant on Clement Street in our neighborhood. It quickly became the place we went to for special occasions and birthdays, a place to give my mom a day off. As I got older, it also became the place I ate when I wanted to get my fix of *mohinga*, a catfish noodle soup and one of my favorite dishes. I kept

returning to Burma Superstar because it served the best Burmese food I could find outside of my mom's kitchen. For nearly five years, I ate at the restaurant twice a week. (Although seemingly every time I ate there, Mr. Wu, the owner, asked me if it was my first time at the restaurant.) When I started dating Joycelyn Lee, she joined me there. Although she is Chinese-American and didn't grow up eating mohinga like I did, it didn't take long for her to become as big a fan of the dish as I was. Yet despite my love for the restaurant, I never would have anticipated that I would end up owning it—and expanding it.

With nudging from Joycelyn, I bought Burma Superstar because I wanted to preserve our favorite restaurant, and I have never taken its success for granted. It makes me happy that our daughter, Mya, loves mohinga as much as we do. Even today, I am amazed at how well Burmese food is received outside of the Burmese community. The popularity of Burma Superstar has given me opportunities to open more restaurants in San Francisco as well as across the bay in Oakland and Alameda. It also inspired me to start importing *laphet*, Burmese fermented tea—the foundation of the restaurant's most popular salad—directly from tea growers in Myanmar's eastern Shan State. Who would have thought that out of all the dishes on our menu, Americans would go nuts for a salad mixed with a dark green savory paste of fermented tea?

Today, more travelers are visiting my former home country. They are eating the curries, noodles, vegetables, and salads as they're served there, and they're coming home wanting more of it. These days, I no longer have to be as hesitant about serving food with shrimp paste and fish sauce as I was when I first bought Burma Superstar. It is one of the reasons that I wanted to do this book: to share not only restaurant dishes but also the home-style food that I grew up with. People are ready for it.

Myanmar is changing quickly too. I fly into Yangon several times a year now. Each time I go,

I see more foreigners, more cell phones—and more cars. A cab ride that used to take thirty minutes can last two hours because of traffic. I sometimes worry that as Myanmar enters the modern world, it will change for the worse. I want the people of Myanmar to have more opportunities to improve their quality of life. I want more people, especially the ones living in rural areas, to have reliable access to electricity and clean water. But I don't want to see the people of Myanmar lose their heritage. I don't want kids there to get so wrapped up in phones and material things that they lose interest in pickup games of soccer—or even stealing the occasional piece of fruit.

The Buddhist religion stresses the importance of giving back to the community, a value that I was raised with. It is one of the reasons that I decided to use some of our profits to rebuild a classroom at a monastery-run orphanage in Bagan, where people travel from all over the world to see the ruins of Myanmar's famous medieval kingdom. There, young boys live as novice monks and study hard (Burmese, Chinese, and English are all mandatory languages), but they also find time to play, using a few rubber bands to entertain each other with magic tricks or kicking a ball around the dusty yard. I hope the new classroom contributes in some small way to their education, but I'm also happy to see that these kids find ways to stay entertained just like I did when I was a kid.

Even in Yangon, where the pace of change is faster than anywhere else in Myanmar, some things do stay more or less the same. While working on this book, I returned to my old neighborhood with a few colleagues as well as my coauthor, Kate Leahy, and photographer, John Lee. It was the first time I had been there since my family moved away. I expected most of it to be torn down and rebuilt. But Tharaphi Street looked almost the same, apart from all of the cars parked in front of the apartment buildings. We came to a door that looked familiar. I knocked, wondering if I could

ask someone if they remembered my family. An older man opened the door, and I started to talk to him. We talked for a few minutes before we realized that we were related: this man was my dad's brother, the basketball uncle, and this was the home where my family once lived.

My aunt was walking home from the market when she saw us standing at the door. Once she realized who I was, she ran inside to pull out a picture of her sons. Like me, they were tall for Burmese men; they looked like they could be my brothers. A few tears welled up in her eyes. These were cousins that I had never met.

Later that week while still in Yangon, our book crew packed into a cab to head across town to a teahouse a friend had recommended. The afternoon downpour had already hit like clockwork—August is prime monsoon season—but even so, we saw kids playing soccer under an on-ramp shielded from the rain. Even though they were barefoot, they had a lot of skill moving the ball; it never flew into traffic. I'll take those kids as a sign that, no matter what comes next, Myanmar's kids will still find ways to have fun, play games, and not take everything too seriously—hopefully, far into the future.

—Desmond Tan

INTRODUCTION: A BREAKOUT STAR

★

When people ask what, exactly, Burma Superstar is, the short answer is to say that it's a popular neighborhood restaurant. Yet, like most restaurants that have been around for a couple of decades, there's a lot more to the story.

Over the past twenty-five years or so, Burma Superstar has evolved into the kind of institution where people wait (and wait) for a table to eat twenty-plus-ingredient salads, samosas in soup, and rich, savory curries. It's morphed into a cultural ambassador, introducing a few unusual Burmese ideas—like eating tea—to American audiences. And it's transformed into a company that hires and trains refugees from Asia with the help of relief organizations. The success of Burma Superstar can't be attributed to any single person. The original owners, the Wu family; Desmond Tan, who bought the restaurant in 2000; Joycelyn Lee, Desmond's wife–turned–business partner; the many cooks, servers, dishwashers, and managers who have worked there throughout the years—all have played important roles.

Yet if you had pegged this restaurant to be a hit from day one, people would have called you crazy.

Burma Superstar opened in 1992 on San Francisco's Clement Street, a corridor of Chinese grocery stores and modest restaurants in the Inner Richmond, the city's other Chinatown. The Wus, a Burmese-Chinese family, took over a Chinese restaurant, added some Burmese dishes, and renamed it Burma Superstar. They wanted a name that connoted a super successful restaurant. In those days, though, there wasn't much demand for a place serving food from a country that no one knew anything about. The restaurant was also on the wrong block. All of the action on Clement Street happened west of 6th Avenue.

Karen Wong, a longtime employee who grew up in the neighborhood, remembers walking by the perennially empty restaurant well before she started working there. No one ever thought of going out to eat on that block, she recalls. The dark interior, with low ceilings and a gazebo encompassing most of the dining room, didn't add curb appeal. Mr. and Mrs. Wu played it safe, keeping a lot of the dishes from the previous restaurant's menu. Along with Burmese curries and soups, there was Mongolian beef, kung pao chicken, and five kinds of egg foo yong. That was what people in the neighborhood wanted.

The San Francisco restaurant scene has always been a competitive one, but during the 1990s, Inner Richmond restaurants competed largely on price over flavor. In order to attract frugal customers (who may only visit the restaurant once), it was common for places on Clement Street to lower their prices to such an extent that the owners could no longer cover operating costs. That fate had struck Burma Superstar. The Wus wanted out of the business. In the fall of 2000, they put the restaurant up for sale.

Desmond and Joycelyn were eating lunch at Burma Superstar on a Saturday when they found out that the restaurant was for sale. All signs pointed to converting Burma Superstar back into a Chinese restaurant. But the restaurant had long become a favorite spot for Desmond and his family. When he had started dating Joycelyn, he introduced the restaurant to her and she soon became a loyal customer. While neither had any experience with restaurants—Desmond ran a tech consulting firm and Joycelyn was a graphic designer—they couldn't stand the idea that their source for mohinga would soon be gone.

Joycelyn encouraged Desmond to buy the place. "How difficult could running a restaurant be?" she said.

He passed along his phone number to a server and said he wanted to talk to someone about buying the business. On Sunday night around 10:00 p.m., Mr. Wu called Desmond.

"Are you really interested in buying the restaurant?" Mr. Wu asked, incredulous. "Don't you want to take a look at it first?"

The next day, Desmond walked through the space. The tiny kitchen was cramped and needed countless improvements, and there was still that gazebo problem in the dining room. But Desmond's main concern about buying Burma Superstar wasn't the physical space. Before taking over the restaurant, he wanted to make sure he could retain the kitchen staff, including Wai K. Law, a Chinese chef whom everyone called Jacky (with a "y")—a tribute to how his cooking skills brought to mind Jackie Chan—and Ma Sein, a woman who grew up

in Yangon. Mr. Wu assured him that the odds were good the staff would stay, especially if Desmond paid them a little more.

By Wednesday, Desmond had signed the deal and brought in his company's office manager to organize the restaurant's accounts. The staff got a raise. Desmond and Joycelyn worked with a fly-by-night ponytailed contractor Desmond met over burritos in the Mission District to give the interior a quick fix (adios, gazebo). When the contractor failed to show up one day (Desmond suspected he headed to Southeast Asia to take part in the expat life), Joycelyn found herself laying tile to finish the job. Not everything changed though. An old chair that no one sat in remained in the kitchen. Joycelyn suggested moving it out—or at least getting a new one—but the cooks protested. It was the ghost chair, and if it were gone, how would the restaurant be hospitable to ghosts? So she let it be. When it came to spirits, it was better to play it safe.

Making money was not the primary objective in buying the restaurant, and Desmond was prepared to take a loss while getting a better sense of the restaurant business. He never intended to quit his day job. Joycelyn wanted to learn how restaurants operated, so she came in after work to wait tables. Desmond arrived later, bussing tables and taking over in the dish pit so the dishwasher could catch the last bus back to Daly City. About four months into owning the restaurant, however, the effects of San Francisco's dot-com bust began to be felt all over the city. When Joycelyn lost her job, she turned her full attention to the restaurant. But this was not a great time to be invested in restaurants, especially one on the sleepy side of 6th Avenue. One night they hit a new low, grossing only $300. Joycelyn was worried. How could this restaurant sustain itself if it couldn't pay its employees?

The answer came in rethinking the menu. Joycelyn began to spend more time in the kitchen, learning how to chop onions and stir-fry rice. When hiring new kitchen employees, she would tell them that they had to be able to chop onions faster than her. Being in the kitchen also exposed her to what the cooks liked to make for their own meals, and she would ask questions. One day it was a noodle salad seasoned with tamarind water. "How many kinds of noodles are in this?" she asked. "Can we make this for customers?" Today, Rainbow Salad—made with more than twenty ingredients—rivals only the Tea Leaf Salad for most popular dish on the menu.

Meanwhile, Desmond used his time washing dishes as an opportunity to see what people were leaving on the plate. It was clear to both Joycelyn and Desmond that many dishes had to go. No more egg foo yong, no more Mongolian beef. No more of a dish called Southeast Asian Chicken served with french fries. Some Burmese dishes were modified too. Instead of making Tea Leaf Salad with shredded cabbage, the old-school way, they made it California-style, with sliced romaine lettuce.

While revamping the menu, they realized they had to do a better job of explaining Burmese food. Everyone had a lot of questions. Is it like Thai food? Indian food? No . . . and yes. Burmese cooking is savory, salty, and tart. Curries are subtle compared with those of neighboring countries, while salads can be enticingly over-the-top with textures and flavors. To make the salads more understandable, Joycelyn and Desmond trained the servers to mix salads tableside and point out each ingredient as they mixed. But even while retooling the menu to focus on Burmese flavors, no one wanted to strip the menu of popular Chinese dishes completely. Today, the stir-fried Chili Lamb remains a perennial favorite.

To expose more people to unfamiliar Burmese fare, Desmond began asking tables if he could order them one dish to see if they liked it. The Tea Leaf Salad became a test. If the table liked it, he would recommend more Burmese dishes, like Pumpkin Pork Stew. And if they didn't, he'd play it safe and suggest Sesame Chicken.

Gradually word got around about other dishes, like Coconut Rice topped with fried onions and Samusa Soup, and by the mid-2000s, hour-long waits for tables were everyday occurrences. The daily crowds that gathered in front of the restaurant grabbed the attention of Lynda Vong, who grew up in the neighborhood and worked at a school down the street. She walked in one day, asked for a job, and has been there ever since. Karen Wong, Lynda's friend from school, also joined the team, becoming the keeper of the wait list. Armed with a flip phone, she quickly learned crowd-control strategies—free hot tea for waiting customers became one solution. So did a hostess podium. Mr. and Mrs. Wu's nephew, Kenneth, also came in on the weekends to help in the kitchen because he thought it was important that more people eat Burmese food.

Every now and again, Desmond would get a call from a Burmese restaurant owner asking him to buy his business. Desmond always said no; one Burma Superstar was enough. Then in 2007 he started talking to an owner of a Burmese restaurant in Alameda, a city on the other side of the Bay Bridge next to Oakland. It was a fifty-seat space along Park Street, the main drag, with a sunny back area shared with a hair salon. The man was ready to sell. Desmond decided to take the chance and test the popularity of Burmese food outside of the Inner Richmond. Chuck Chin was one of the first employees hired. A Chinese cook originally from Yangon who had spent more than a decade cooking in Texas before moving to Oakland, Chuck heard about the job opening through his brother, was promptly hired, and has been there ever since.

While working on the Alameda restaurant, Desmond found another potential restaurant space on Telegraph Avenue in Oakland's Temescal neighborhood and nabbed it. But by then it was 2009, the economy was in another downturn, and, like in 2001, nobody was eating out. Plus, the Telegraph Avenue location had all kinds of things wrong with

it. A tree blocked the front entrance. Neighboring eateries had security issues. And the restaurant space—as Desmond learned after the fact—wasn't even legally a restaurant space. Osama Asif, one of the restaurant's managers, had to straighten that all out with the city of Oakland. To make matters more ominous, opening manager Tiyo Bestia received a letter from a neighbor calling the staff crazy for wanting to open a restaurant in that cursed space. But the restaurant was a runaway success. That pesky tree out front? A bench was built around it where people could sit and wait for a table. (The neighbor later apologized for writing the letter.)

A lot of people put chefs on pedestals, but everyone is important in Burma Superstar's operations. The restaurants' staffs are multiethnic and multilingual, and all have their own traditions. Clement Street's restaurant is like a tight-knit family that gets together after hours at the restaurant for occasional hot pot nights. At Oakland and Alameda, many employees—both in the front and the back of the house—are siblings. Some are refugees from Myanmar and other Asian countries. Alex Naitun Thawng (Nin for short), the kitchen manager at the Oakland restaurant, and Nang Khan Cin (nicknamed Afoo), who co-runs the Alameda restaurant with Chuck, found their way to Burma Superstar through the International Rescue Committee, a refugee relief organization that helps with resettlement. Both managers are Chin, one of Myanmar's numerous ethnic groups. Kitchen meetings at all of the restaurants are games of telephone, with words translated into everything from Chinese and Burmese to Chin and Spanish. The multicultural backdrop of the restaurants parallels the melting pot within Myanmar, which is one of the most ethnically diverse countries in Asia.

It is true that attaching "Superstar" to a restaurant's name is an audacious thing to do. It's even out of character, considering that there is no one star player—no chef, owner, manager, cook, or server—who can take all of the credit for the

success of the restaurants. But there is another rising star deserving of attention, and it's Myanmar itself. After decades of military rule, the country held its first democratic elections in 2015. For many Burmese employees at the restaurants, this is the first time in their lives that they have had reason to hope for a better future for the relatives they left behind. On a less serious level, political reform is making it possible to dig deeper into Burmese food, whether it's by visiting the source of the country's best fermented tea leaves (see "Eat Your Tea," page 143) or simply by exploring regions that were once closed to foreigners.

This book is a starting point. We've only scratched the surface.

WHAT IS BURMESE FOOD?

If you head down Pansodan Street in Yangon's
historic downtown district, the view of the
century-old colonial architecture is often
obscured by makeshift stalls serving samosas,
hand-mixed noodle salads, and steaming bowls
of *mohinga*, a fish noodle soup that is, for all
intents and purposes, Myanmar's national dish.

This scene of street stalls is repeated all over the city. In the morning and late afternoon, tea shops fill with workers downing their first cup of tea brewed the color of burnt caramel and lightened with condensed and evaporated milks. For lunch at a popular restaurant like Feel, customers point at dishes set out on the counter and then sit down and wait as servers bring small plates to the table in rapid-fire fashion. To escape the afternoon heat, locals pop into shops serving sweetened yogurt drinks or a "heart cooler"—coconut milk served over agar jelly, tapioca pearls, and ice. Before dinner, people line up in front of vendors frying up the Burmese answer to tempura. Like the rest of the country, the city grows quiet at night, with the exception of 19th Street, which turns into an open-air market where you can pick and choose from stalls offering skewers of whole fish, squid, pork intestine, or mushrooms. Pitchers of Myanmar beer tide over groups of customers while the stalls grill selections.

Eating in Yangon means sampling a range of culinary traditions, from regional ethnic foods to dishes adapted from neighboring countries, especially China and India. No matter which heritage hits the table, one thing is certain: it's easy to find a dish—or several—that you can't wait to eat again.

Looking at a map, it's tempting to tuck Myanmar in with the rest of Southeast Asia. Yet the food of Myanmar has its own distinctions. It is savory, occasionally salty, sometimes sour, and often unapologetically funky. Slow-cooked onions and garlic, ground chiles and turmeric, and shrimp paste are the building blocks of countless dishes. Tamarind water is just as important as lime juice for adding acidity to a salad or soup. And breaking up all of those flavors is crunch: fried split peas, fried garlic, crushed peanuts, and toasted chickpea flour are mixed into just about everything.

Burmese food also has a very familiar feel to it, thanks to liberal borrowing from neighbors throughout the centuries. In the geopolitical sense, Myanmar has long occupied a strategically valuable location between India and China. And while modern Burmese history is best known for isolationism, the country wasn't always so cut off from the rest of the world. Even the origin story that all Burmese schoolkids are taught speaks to the influence of outsiders: Abhiraja, a prince of the Sakayan clan from India, founded the kingdom of Tagaung. The legend maintains that all of Burma's kings could trace their lineage back to Tagaung, which today is a dusty village near the Burmese city of Mandalay. India, where Buddhism originated, continued to influence Burmese high society in ancient and modern times. And when Bagan, the country's famous Buddhist kingdom, reached its height of power in 1100 AD, many of the ideas in art, architecture, and language it was absorbing came from South India—the cultural capital of South Asia at the time.

Yet it wasn't all about peace and love. Burmese kings also fended off invasions by Mongols and sparked battles with Siam. Closer to home, rival Mon and Rakhine kingdoms and city-states posed threats at different times.

One of the results of a tumultuous history is an unusually diverse country. Myanmar's population comprises 135 ethnic groups officially recognized by the government—and many more that go unrecognized. And while today the Bamar people (formerly called Burman by the British) make up the majority, the largest minority groups, particularly the Mon, Rakhine, Kayin, Chin, and Shan people, have played significant roles in shaping Myanmar's food traditions.

In modern times, outsiders have also had a substantial impact on Burmese food, especially in Yangon. The British captured the city during the First Anglo-Burmese War ending in 1826. After the Second Anglo-Burmese war in the mid-nineteenth century, the city became a hub for commerce and later was named the colonial capital. British colonists called it "Rangoon" because that was easier for them to pronounce. By the early twentieth century, Rangoon was booming, drawing in everyone from Scottish traders to Armenian hoteliers. Even today, the interiors of the remaining colonial buildings in downtown Yangon are striking spaces, with tiles from England and steel beams from Scotland.

In 1927, Rangoon surpassed New York as the greatest immigrant port in the world, wrote Thant Myint-U, the grandson of former UN Secretary-General U Thant, in his book *The River of Lost Footsteps: A Personal History of Burma*. Ancient golden pagodas—from downtown's Sule Pagoda to the gleaming grounds of the famous Shwedagon—coexisted with churches, mosques, Hindu temples, and a synagogue or two. In part because of British rule, roughly half the city's population was Indian, and the popularity of certain Indian dishes, from biryanis to samosas, became widespread. During this time, the Chinese population in Rangoon also grew. Chinese cooking in Rangoon meant turmeric and ground chiles as well as noodles, soy sauce, and pickled greens. These two cultures also had a lasting impact on what Burmese food is today.

So what does it mean to eat Burmese? It means eating cultural mashups in the best possible sense, from Chinese-style noodles and Indian-style soups and flatbreads to the simple curries, vegetables, and salads made popular in the countryside. It also means sampling foods from ethnic groups little known outside of Myanmar. While Yangon is regaining some of its international cachet (there are now sushi bars, Korean chain restaurants, and even Kentucky Fried Chicken), some of its most popular places serve regional food. Today, you can find both humble and fancy spots serving yellow tofu from Shan State and large open-air restaurants serving spicy seafood dishes from Rakhine State. Fortunately, these flavors travel well outside of the country and are worth making at home on the other side of the world.

The Recipes

The dishes in this book reflect this idea of a great big Asian melting pot. While the recipes are all linked to Burma Superstar in some way, they are not exclusively from the restaurant's menu. Some are from trips to Myanmar and others are from home cooks in Myanmar and San Francisco. Is everything in this book authentically Burmese (whatever that means)? No. This collection of recipes is a little more eclectic and a little more personal, representative of how Burmese cooking came to be interpreted through the lens of a Burmese restaurant in San Francisco. The goal in this book is also to include dishes that taste good together and are made with ingredients that are widely available to home cooks, even if some require a little sleuthing.

Serving a Burma Superstar Meal

Eating a meal in Myanmar means choosing from a lot of little dishes. Everyone at the table gets a little cup of brothy soup and a plate with a big scoop of rice in the center. Then you help yourself from a bunch of small plates, which include curries, cooked vegetables and beans, and salads. In America, portions are heartier. In this book, portion sizes run large enough that you can put together a meal with a curry, some rice, and a side of vegetables or a salad, and it will serve four people comfortably. If you make several dishes over the course of a week, leftovers generally keep well and can be served a second time around. The exception to the multidish style of eating in this book are the soups, like *mohinga*, which are hearty enough to be a meal on their own.

When deciding what to cook for your friends or family, heed the advice of Yuncon Tu, a longtime server at the Alameda restaurant. He recommends mixing and matching Burmese with Chinese dishes—making one curry and one stir-fry and pairing them with a side of vegetables to give a meal the optimal balance of textures and flavors. Pork Curry can be served with Fiery Tofu and Wok-Tossed Pea Shoots, or Chili Lamb with Ginger Salad and *Nan Gyi Thoke* (coconut chicken curry with rice noodles). And *platha*, a buttery layered flatbread similar to Indian roti, goes with pretty much everything. When it comes to setting the table for a meal, you can offer chopsticks—which are doled out at noodle shops and roadside stops in states near the Chinese border—but it's far more common (and practical) to provide guests with a fork and a spoon. In Myanmar, the job of the fork is to push the food into the spoon, not the other way around.

Where to Start

To get familiar with ingredient combinations and cooking methods used in this book, start with a curry from the first chapter and make a pot of rice to eat alongside it. (Plain and coconut rice recipes are both available in the Rice and Basics section in the back of the book.) Then add a side of vegetables. When you're getting into a groove, tackle the chapters later in the book, such as noodles, soups, and salads. Many noodles and salads (and noodle salads) require components that you can make ahead and use in multiple recipes—like fried onions, fried garlic, and fried yellow split peas. Along with the rice, those recipes are gathered in the Rice and Basics section so they are easy to flip to when needed.

The recipes measure certain ingredients, like onions and garlic, in cups and tablespoons. There is just too much ambiguity around the size of a "medium yellow onion." But don't get too hung up on measuring out every last ingredient to the quarter teaspoon. Burmese recipes are never ruined by adding an extra tablespoon of minced garlic or quarter cup of sliced onions. And when in doubt, add tamarind salt. While working on this book, we found that there were few things that the mildly tangy salt could not improve.

Start cooking

RICE

+

CURRY

then add some vegetables

NEXT, TRY

NOODLES, SALADS, SOUPS

THE LAY OF THE LAND

Sandwiched in between India (and the Bay of Bengal) and China, Myanmar lies within Asia's monsoon region. Some parts of the country get parched in the dry season, which begins around October, and drenched in the rainy season, which starts up around June. In this climate, mangoes, papayas, guavas, durian, water spinach, okra, beans, and chiles grow easily.

In the eastern Shan State, which borders China and Thailand, cauliflower, cabbage, ginger, eggplant, mustard greens, garlic, onions, carrots, tomatoes, and potatoes are common crops. Much of what's grown there is trucked into Mandalay, the country's hub for agricultural trade.

A little more than half of Myanmar is the Ayeyarwady River Valley. The upper portion of the valley is the dry zone, where farmers grow staple crops such as sesame seeds and peanuts for cooking oil. Here, the cooking is simple and direct, stemming from the Bamar people,

Myanmar's dominant ethnic group. Directly west of the plains and walled off by mountains is Rakhine State, where the food is much spicier and more reminiscent of the food of southern India. With a long stretch of coastline, ocean-caught seafood is more common in Rakhine State than inland, where most people prefer cooking with freshwater fish.

North of Rakhine State is the rugged Chin State, a rural area known for its main river, the Chindwin, which links up with the Ayeyarwady. There, hills and mountains make rice cultivation challenging, and corn and millet are the more common grains.

South of Yangon, it's a steamy scene more suited for growing rice. The Ayeyarwady Delta was the most prolific rice-producing region in the world before World War II. Shrimp paste is used more frequently here than upcountry. Farther south is the Mon State, where the main city, Mawlamyine—formerly called Moulmein—is reputed to have some of the best cooks in the country. (It's said that mohinga originated here.) South of Mawlamyine is Myanmar's skinny tail of coastline that hugs the Thai border. It's largely remote, though that's bound to change as tourists discover its beaches.

CURRIES AND SLOW-COOKED DISHES

Alex Naitun Thawng—"Nin"—heads the kitchen
at Oakland's Burma Superstar. There, he makes curries
by the stockpot.

To ensure no bits of onion scorch on the bottom of the pot during the process, he stirs the onions with a wok spatula fashioned with a long wooden handle, giving the spatula the effect of a paddle. Once the onions are soft, with most of their water cooked out, Nin builds up flavor in layers, starting with the garlic, following with the chicken, coconut milk, and fish sauce, and finishing with generous pinches of curry powder and cayenne. The curry is ready when bits of paprika-red oil rise to the surface, but it always tastes better when left to rest for a few hours. Ask Nin, who is from Myanmar's Chin State, what he'd do if he were making curry for himself and the answer is easy: bump up the heat with a lot of Thai chiles.

Compared with spicy and elaborate Indian and Thai curries, Burmese curries are mildly spiced, deeply savory, and easy to make at home. Whether featuring meat, fish, or vegetables, the curries all share the same rhythm and bass. Start by sweating the onions or shallots in oil and then add garlic and sometimes ginger and lemongrass (especially if the curry features fish or shrimp). Nearly all of the curries use turmeric and some sort of ground chile to spice things up. All of this is cooked gently until the oil "returns," by rising back to the surface.

The oil used in Burmese cooking is neutral in flavor, but it's the quantity of oil that gets people talking. There's a reason the Burmese go heavy on oil. Traditionally, access to refrigeration was limited, so sealing off a curry with a layer of oil was a way to protect it from contaminants. Starting a curry with oil also makes the onions and garlic cook more evenly without as much risk of burning them. And in dishes like Burmese Chicken Biryani (page 30), the oil used to fry the onions is used again later to flavor the dish. Today, many urban Burmese cook with less oil or ladle extra oil out of the pot after cooking the onions. The recipes in this book offer middle ground, using more oil than is typical in America but less oil than would be traditional in Myanmar.

When making the curries in this book, allow time for cooking the water out of the onions so the oil returns to the surface. All spice levels are easy to control: dial up more heat when you add the garlic by throwing in some minced Thai chiles or a couple of small dried chiles when you add the garlic. For less heat, switch to seeded, minced jalapeños and omit the cayenne and dried chiles. Serving the curries with plain rice does a great deal to cut the heat and richness.

While eggs and okra are the headliner ingredients of this simple curry, don't overlook the virtues of the simple sauce. Made from slow-cooked shallots, garlic, and tomatoes and a generous amount of turmeric, it's so popular that the staff at sister restaurant Burma Love spoons it alone over rice. Shallots (or onions) are used in two places—minced for the sauce and sliced for texture. In Myanmar, cooks fry hard-boiled eggs to help them hold their shape in this classic curry, but not everyone is a fan of the ensuing rubbery texture. Frying isn't actually necessary: adding the eggs at the end preserves their shape just fine.

EGG AND OKRA CURRY

SERVES 4; 6 AS PART OF A LARGER MEAL

¼ cup canola oil

¾ cup finely diced shallots or yellow onion

¼ cup minced garlic

1 to 3 Thai chiles, sliced crosswise, or ½ jalapeño, seeded and minced

½ teaspoon turmeric

½ teaspoon paprika

¼ teaspoon cayenne

1 teaspoon salt

3 cups diced Roma tomatoes (about 6 tomatoes)

10½ ounces okra (about 15), tops trimmed, cut into 2-inch pieces

1 cup sliced shallots or yellow onion

1 tablespoon fish sauce

4 hard-boiled eggs (see sidebar)

1 cup cilantro sprigs, for garnish

In a 4-quart pot, heat the oil over medium-high heat. Stir in the diced shallots and cook until softened, about 1 minute (this will take a few more minutes if using onion). Add the garlic and chiles, decrease the heat to low, and cook, stirring frequently, until the garlic has begun to turn golden but has not started to brown, 1 to 2 minutes. (If the garlic starts to stick to the bottom of the pot, turn off the heat for a minute and stir, letting the garlic cook off the heat to avoid scorching it.)

Stir in the turmeric, paprika, cayenne, and salt. Add the tomatoes and cook over medium-low heat, stirring occasionally, until the tomatoes lose their shape and form a sauce, about 10 minutes. Stir in the okra, sliced shallots, and fish sauce and cook for 2 to 3 minutes more or until the okra is just tender but not mushy. Season with more fish sauce or salt if desired.

Cut the eggs in half. Nestle the eggs, cut-side up, in the pot and bring to a simmer. Gently stir the curry, ensuring that the eggs hold their shape, until the eggs are heated through. Include 1 or 2 egg halves in each serving. Serve with a bowl of cilantro sprigs at the table.

HOW TO HARD-BOIL EGGS

Older eggs are easier to peel than fresh eggs, so if you're making a lot of hard-boiled eggs, it's not a bad idea to buy them a week in advance.

To hard-boil eggs, place cold eggs in a pot and cover with cold water. Bring the pot to a boil, cover, and set a timer for 10 minutes. Have a bowl of ice water and a spider or slotted spoon handy. Once the timer goes off, use the spider to lift the eggs out of the hot water and into the ice bath. Peel when cool enough to handle.

Burmese cooks will tell you to always cook fish curries with ginger—and sometimes lemongrass—to kill off fishy aromas. While ginger serves this practical purpose, it also brightens up the base of slow-cooked onions and garlic. On the West Coast, rockfish is an affordable fish that works well in this curry. But catfish or any other mild, white-fleshed fish will do as well.

SIMPLE FISH CURRY

Trim away any bones from the fish fillets. (Rockfish fillets often have a set of ribs running halfway down the center. Simply slice down both sides of the bones to cut them out.) Cut the fish into ½- to 1-inch pieces. Transfer to a bowl and use your hands to mix the fish with the salt and curry powder. Let sit at room temperature while you prepare the other ingredients.

In a 6-quart pot, heat the oil over medium-high heat. Add the onions and cook, stirring occasionally, until the onions have softened and the edges start to brown, about 4 minutes. Add the garlic, ginger, and lemongrass and cook until the garlic is golden brown, 1 minute more. Stir in the chiles and shrimp paste and cook for 1 minute.

Stir in the paprika, cayenne, and turmeric and add the tomatoes. Cook, stirring often, until the sauce begins to thicken, about 15 minutes. If the tomatoes are on the dry side and do not release much water, add about ½ cup of water to help them cook down.

Stir in the fish and fish sauce and cook gently for 5 minutes or until the fish is cooked through. Add the tamarind water and taste, adding more salt or fish sauce if desired. Let the flavors meld for 10 minutes before serving.

Soak the shallots in cold water for about 5 minutes. Drain. Serve the curry with the shallots at the table.

SERVES 4; 6 AS PART OF A LARGER MEAL

1½ pounds skinless rockfish fillets or catfish fillets

1 teaspoon salt

½ teaspoon Madras curry powder

¼ cup canola oil

1 cup finely diced yellow onion

2 tablespoons minced garlic

2 tablespoons minced ginger

2 tablespoons minced lemongrass (see page 228; optional)

1 to 2 Thai chiles, finely sliced, or ½ jalapeño, minced

1 tablespoon shrimp paste (see page 238)

½ teaspoon paprika

½ teaspoon cayenne

½ teaspoon turmeric

4 cups diced Roma tomatoes (about 8 tomatoes)

1 tablespoon fish sauce

2 tablespoons Tamarind Water (page 218)

½ cup sliced shallots, for garnish (optional)

In Myanmar, river prawns can grow to the size of lobsters—big enough to be cut in half and grilled. But most shrimp—a term that tends to be used interchangeably with prawns in Myanmar—are cooked into curries like this one: a simple, "dry" curry, meaning that most of the juices have been cooked off, leaving behind concentrated flavors. Made with large headless shrimp, this is a satisfying curry with rice and vegetables. However, if you're fortunate enough to find shrimp or prawns with the head on (see sidebar), this curry becomes extra special: the oils from the heads give the dish a deeper red hue.

TOMATO SHRIMP CURRY

SERVES 4; 6 AS PART OF A LARGER MEAL

1½ pounds large shrimp (16–20 or 20–25 per pound), peeled and deveined

1 tablespoon fish sauce

½ teaspoon salt

3 tablespoons canola oil

2 cups finely diced yellow onion

2 tablespoons minced garlic

1 tablespoon minced ginger

1 to 2 Thai chiles, thinly sliced

1 teaspoon shrimp paste (see page 238)

1 teaspoon paprika

½ teaspoon turmeric

2 cups diced Roma tomatoes (about 4 tomatoes)

1 cup cilantro sprigs, for garnish

1 lime or lemon, cut into wedges, for garnish

In a bowl, use your hands to mix the shrimp with the fish sauce and salt. Let sit at room temperature while you prepare the other ingredients.

In a 6-quart pot, heat the oil over medium-high heat. Add the onions and cook, stirring occasionally, until the onions have softened and the edges start to brown, about 6 minutes. Stir in the garlic and ginger and cook until the garlic is golden brown, 1 minute more. Stir in the chiles and shrimp paste and cook for another minute or two.

Stir in the paprika and turmeric and then add the tomatoes. Cook, stirring often, until the tomatoes lose their shape and soften and the sauce is thick enough to stand up on a spoon, about 7 minutes. If the tomatoes are on the dry side and do not release much water, add about ¼ cup of water to help them cook down.

Stir in the shrimp and gently coat in the sauce. Cook gently for 3 to 5 minutes or until the shrimp are cooked through. Taste, adding more salt or fish sauce if desired. Serve with bowls of cilantro and lime wedges at the table.

HOW TO PEEL AND DEVEIN
HEAD-ON PRAWNS

Use a pair of scissors to trim away the legs and tip of the tail. Peel off the shell around the body and tail. Gently pull off the head's shell and remove any greenish parts, but leave any red goop you find and keep some of the shell on the sides of the prawn's body if possible—it looks vaguely like ribs. (Leaving these "ribs" in place will increase the depth of prawn flavor in the curry.) With a paring knife, slice the prawn's tail down the back to expose the thin digestive-tract vein. Pull it out and discard.

If you make only one curry from this book, let it be this one. Simple, satisfying, and made with ingredients that are easy to find, Coconut Chicken Curry is a workhorse in the Burma Superstar kitchen. At the restaurant, it's the base for noodle dish Nan Gyi Thoke (page 98) and the dip for Platha (page 181), a buttery flatbread. Alone, it's a satisfying meal with rice. For best results, cook the curry the day before serving to give the flavors time to soak into the chicken. This recipe makes about 7 cups, so you can freeze any leftovers to make Nan Gyi Thoke or serve with platha down the road.

COCONUT CHICKEN CURRY

SERVES 4; 6 AS PART OF A LARGER MEAL

2½ pounds boneless, skinless chicken thighs

1 tablespoon paprika

½ teaspoon turmeric

2 teaspoons salt

⅓ cup canola oil

3 cups finely diced yellow onion

2 tablespoons minced garlic

1 (13½-ounce) can unsweetened coconut milk

1½ tablespoons fish sauce

1½ cups water

1 teaspoon Madras curry powder

½ teaspoon cayenne

1 cup cilantro sprigs, for garnish

1 lime or lemon, cut into wedges, for garnish

Trim the chicken thighs of excess fat and cut into ½- to 1-inch pieces. Transfer to a bowl and use your hands to mix with the paprika, turmeric, and salt. Let the chicken marinate at room temperature while you prepare the other ingredients, or refrigerate it overnight.

In a 6-quart pot, heat the oil over medium-high heat. Stir in the onions, decrease the heat to medium-low and cook gently, stirring often to prevent scorching, for 10 minutes. Add the garlic and continue to cook until most of the water from the onions has been cooked out and a glossy layer of oil has risen to the surface, about 5 minutes more.

Add the chicken and stir to release the spices into the onions. Pour in the coconut milk, increase the heat, and bring to a near boil. Let the coconut milk simmer briskly for about 4 minutes to thicken a bit. Decrease the heat to medium-low and add the fish sauce. Stir in the water and bring the pot back to a near boil. The broth will thin out as the chicken starts to release its juices.

Lower to a gentle simmer and cook, stirring occasionally, until the chicken is tender, 50 to 55 minutes. Droplets of paprika-red oil will rise to the surface. Stir in the curry powder and cayenne, simmer briefly, and remove from the heat.

If time permits, let the curry sit for at least 20 minutes before serving. This allows the chicken to soak in more flavor as the curry cools. Bring to a simmer before serving and taste, adding more salt or fish sauce if desired. Serve with bowls of cilantro and lime wedges at the table.

Dried beans and lentils—dal—are staples in Myanmar, where they are served slow-cooked or fried until crispy. In this recipe, they deepen the curry's savory flavors and make it more protein-rich. To prepare the split peas, soak them overnight and then add them when the curry is halfway finished. If you don't get a chance to soak them, play catch-up by simmering the split peas with 2 cups of water in a separate pot for 20 minutes while the curry cooks. Drain the split peas and add them to the curry when the chicken is nearly done.

CHICKEN DAL CURRY

SERVES 4; 6 AS PART OF A LARGER MEAL

½ cup yellow split peas

2½ pounds bone-in chicken thighs, skin removed

1 tablespoon paprika

½ teaspoon turmeric

1 tablespoon fish sauce

2 teaspoons salt

⅓ cup canola oil

1-ounce piece ginger, peeled and sliced crosswise into thick pieces

2½ cups finely diced yellow onion

⅓ cup finely minced garlic

1 to 3 Thai chiles, thinly sliced (optional)

Cover the split peas with at least 1 inch of water and soak overnight. The next day, drain the split peas and keep on hand for the curry.

Cut the chicken thighs into 2-inch pieces with some pieces containing bone and others without. Transfer to a bowl and use your hands to mix with the paprika, turmeric, fish sauce, and salt. Let the chicken marinate at room temperature while you prepare the other ingredients, or refrigerate it overnight.

In a 6-quart pot, heat all but 1 tablespoon of the oil over medium-high heat. Add the ginger and cook until the edges become lightly browned, 2 minutes. Add the onions and cook, stirring often to prevent scorching, until the onions have softened, about 4 minutes. Stir in the garlic, chiles, and bay leaves, decrease the heat to medium-low, and cook gently until most of the water from the onions has been cooked out and a glossy layer of oil has risen to the surface, about 10 minutes. Transfer the contents of the pot to a bowl and give the pot a quick wipe to ensure no bits of onion or garlic remain.

Add the remaining 1 tablespoon of oil to the pot and heat over medium heat. Add the chicken, distributing the pieces in a single layer if the pot is wide enough. Increase the heat to medium high and let the chicken get a little color on it (but watch carefully so the bottom of the pot doesn't blacken), 2 to 3 minutes. Return the onion paste to the pot, add the water, and bring the pot to a boil.

Lower to a gentle simmer and cook, stirring occasionally, until the chicken is nearly tender, about 40 minutes. Stir in the soaked yellow split peas, curry powder, and garam masala and cook for 30 minutes more. (If the split peas have been cooked separately, add them in the last 10 minutes of cooking.) Remove from the heat.

If time permits, let the curry sit for at least 20 minutes before serving. This allows the chicken to soak in more flavor as the curry cools. Bring to a simmer before serving, and taste, adding more salt or fish sauce if desired. Serve with bowls of cilantro and lime wedges at the table.

2 bay leaves

3 cups water

1 teaspoon Madras curry powder

½ teaspoon Garam Masala (page 216; optional)

1 cup cilantro sprigs, for garnish

1 lime or lemon, cut into wedges, for garnish

Called *dan bauk* in Myanmar, this Burmese answer to Indian biryani is a favorite dish among past and present residents of Yangon, where some restaurants specialize in it. Combining tender spiced chicken and fluffy rice, it's the ultimate comfort food. Pa Bawi, who runs the kitchen at sister restaurant Burma Love in San Francisco's Mission District, says this is the dish he missed the most when he moved to the United States. This version has been adapted to be more of a chicken-rice casserole. The basmati rice is layered with marinated chicken, and everything is infused with the sweet flavors of fried onions. To extend the biryani to serve six people, cut the chicken thighs from the drumsticks before cooking and serve Ginger Salad (page 128) and some Green Mango Pickle (page 222) on the side.

BURMESE CHICKEN BIRYANI

SERVES 4; 6 AS PART OF A LARGER MEAL

Chicken

4 bone-in, skin-on whole chicken legs, thighs attached (about 2½ pounds)

2 tablespoons whole-milk regular or Greek yogurt

1 tablespoon salt

1 teaspoon paprika

1 teaspoon Madras curry powder

1 teaspoon Garam Masala (page 216)

¼ teaspoon turmeric

Rice

1½ cups basmati rice

In a large bowl, use your hands to mix the chicken with the yogurt, salt, paprika, curry powder, garam masala, and turmeric. Let the chicken marinate at room temperature for up to 1 hour while you prepare the other ingredients, or refrigerate it overnight.

Place the bottom rack on the lowest level in the oven and remove the upper rack or move it to the highest rung to make room for a 6-quart Dutch oven or deep saucepan. Preheat the oven to 350°F.

Wash the rice well in 3 to 4 changes of water. Drain it in a fine-mesh strainer and hang the strainer over a pot on the stove while you fry the onions. (The heat from the stove will help the rice dry.)

To fry the onions, line a plate with paper towels. Put a strainer over a bowl. In a skillet, heat the oil over medium heat for 1 to 2 minutes (it shouldn't be scorching hot). Add the onion slices and fry, stirring often. Within a minute or two, decrease the heat to medium-low and continue to fry, stirring often, until golden brown, 18 to 20 minutes. You are close when you notice that fewer bubbles gather around the sides of the onions. Remove from the heat and pour the oil through the strainer; reserve the oil. Give the strainer a good shake and then spread the fried onions over the paper towels.

To brown the chicken, put 2 tablespoons of the onion frying oil in the Dutch oven or deep saucepan and heat over medium heat. Nestle the chicken legs and thighs into the Dutch oven, skin-side down, and lightly brown, 3 to 4 minutes. Turn the pieces over. If the skin sticks to the bottom, it might need to cook a little longer; but if you're worried it's getting too dark, pull it up. If some skin sticks, that's okay. Brown the other side, lowering the heat if necessary to keep the bottom from scorching. Transfer the chicken to a plate. Pour in some water to deglaze the Dutch oven and dislodge burned bits of marinade, if necessary. Pour out the water and wipe the Dutch oven dry.

To season and cook the rice, heat the Dutch oven over medium-high heat. Add 2 more tablespoons of the onion frying oil to the pot. Stir in the garlic and ginger and cook for 1 minute. Add the cardamom, cloves, bay leaves, cinnamon, cumin, coriander, paprika, turmeric, and salt. Stir in the rice and cook, stirring constantly, until the kernels are well coated in the spices and slightly translucent around the edges. Turn off the heat. Stir in the raisins and fried onions.

Nestle the chicken into the rice. Bring 2¼ cups water to a boil and pour over the chicken and rice. Cover the Dutch oven and transfer to the oven. Bake for 50 minutes to 1 hour. Remove the lid and check the chicken: it should be tender when pierced with a fork. The top layer of rice may look dry, but don't worry; it will continue to steam and soften.

Let the biryani sit on the stovetop, covered, for 20 minutes before serving. Serve the chicken with the rice spooned alongside.

Fried Onions

½ cup canola oil

2 cups thinly sliced onion

Rice Seasoning

2 tablespoons minced garlic

1 tablespoon minced ginger

6 green cardamom pods, lightly crushed

4 cloves

3 bay leaves

1 cinnamon stick (about 1½ inches)

1 teaspoon cumin seeds

½ teaspoon coriander seeds

1 teaspoon paprika

½ teaspoon turmeric

½ teaspoon salt

½ cup golden raisins (optional)

Steve Lopas of Ale Industries, the Oakland brewery that makes Burma Superstar's Burma Ale, says Pumpkin Pork Stew is his favorite dish on the menu. He has a very good reason for liking the stew: it's a slam-dunk pairing it with Ale Industries' unhopped Golden State of Mind beer—and Burma Ale, of course. The so-called pumpkin in this dish is kabocha squash, a variety with orange flesh and dark green skin. It is sold year-round in Asian markets and is also often available in other grocery stores in fall and winter. (Butternut squash can be used in its place.) Kabocha squash varies significantly in size, but the good news is that if you have extra, the squash keeps in the refrigerator for a couple of weeks even after it's been cut open. The skin can be hard to peel with a vegetable peeler, but leaving a few stripes of green is perfectly acceptable. If planning to serve the stew the day after making it, keep the pumpkin separate from the pork until you reheat. (Cooked this way, the pumpkin also makes a nice vegetarian side dish with stir-fries.)

PUMPKIN PORK STEW

SERVES 4; 6 AS PART OF A LARGER MEAL

Pumpkin

1 pound kabocha squash (about ¼ of a medium squash), peeled and seeded

2 tablespoons canola oil

2 tablespoons minced garlic

2 tablespoons minced ginger

½ teaspoon turmeric

½ teaspoon salt

To cook the pumpkin, cut the squash into wedges about 1 inch thick. If the wedges are longer than 4 inches, cut them in half crosswise. In a saucepan or pot big enough to fit the pumpkin, heat the oil over medium heat. Add the garlic and ginger and cook, stirring often, until the garlic is golden but before it turns brown, about 1 minute. Stir in the turmeric and remove from the heat. Nestle the pumpkin wedges in the pot and pour in enough water to cover (at least 3½ cups). Add salt. Bring the pot to a boil, then lower to a gentle simmer and cook until the pumpkin is almost tender when pierced with a fork, 10 to 15 minutes. Let the pumpkin cool to room temperature in the cooking water; reserve the water.

To make the pork stew, trim away the sinew from the pork, but leave some of the fat; it will add richness to the stew. Cut the pork into ½- to 1-inch pieces. Transfer to a bowl and use your hands to mix with the salt and turmeric. Let the pork marinate at room temperature while you prepare the other ingredients, or refrigerate it overnight.

In a 6-quart pot, heat the oil over medium heat. Add the onions and cook for 4 minutes, stirring often to prevent scorching. Stir in the ginger, garlic, and chiles and cook until most of the water from the

CONTINUED

Pork Stew

2 pounds boneless pork shoulder

----

2 teaspoons salt

----

1 teaspoon turmeric

⅓ cup canola oil

----

3 cups finely diced yellow onion

----

3 tablespoons minced ginger

----

2 tablespoons minced garlic

----

2 to 3 Thai chiles, thinly sliced
(optional)

----

1 teaspoon Madras curry powder

1½ tablespoons fish sauce (optional)

½ cup mint leaves, for garnish

½ cup cilantro sprigs, for garnish

----

1 lime or lemon, cut into wedges,
for garnish

----

onions has been cooked out and a glossy layer of oil has risen to the surface, about 10 minutes.

Add the pork and stir to coat. Ladle in 3 cups of the pumpkin cooking water (if short on pumpkin water, add tap water to make up the difference). Bring to a boil and then lower to a gentle simmer and cook, stirring occasionally, until the meat is tender when pierced with a fork, about 1½ hours.

Stir in the curry powder and fish sauce, and add the pumpkin and ½ cup of the pumpkin (or tap) water. Simmer gently until the sauce coats each piece of meat and the stew has thickened (it should not be soupy), about 10 minutes.

Ideally, let the stew sit for 20 minutes before serving to let the flavors meld. Bring to a simmer before serving and taste, adding more salt or fish sauce if desired. Serve with bowls of mint, cilantro, and lime wedges at the table.

For this vegetarian alternative to Pumpkin Pork Stew, think Burmese curry, California-style. A few pinches of Tamarind Salt (page 217) curbs sweetness, but a splash of fish sauce (if you're flexitarian) does the job too. Or leave the tofu out and serve the pumpkin on its own as a vegetable side dish. To hit home the California angle, serve the stew with Brown Coconut Rice (page 206).

PUMPKIN TOFU STEW

Line a plate with paper towels. Cut the tofu into 1-inch cubes and scatter on the paper towels to drain.

Soak the ½ cup of sliced onions in cold water for about 5 minutes. Drain.

In a 6-quart pot, heat the oil over medium heat. Add the diced onions and cook, stirring often to prevent scorching, until softened, about 4 minutes. Stir in the garlic, ginger, and fresh and dried chiles, and cook until the onions are completely soft and starting to turn golden, about 6 minutes more.

Add the pumpkin, turmeric, paprika, salt, and tamarind salt and stir to coat. Pour in the water and bring to a boil. Lower to a gentle simmer and cook, stirring occasionally, until the pumpkin is tender when pierced with a knife, about 20 minutes.

Stir in the tofu, garam masala, and a splash of water if the pot looks dry. Simmer gently until the sauce coats each piece of tofu and the stew has thickened (it should not be soupy), about 5 minutes.

Ideally, let the stew sit for at least 10 minutes before serving to let the flavors come together. Bring to a simmer before serving, and taste, adding more salt or tamarind salt if desired. Serve with bowls of sliced onion, cilantro, and lime wedges at the table.

SERVES 4; 6 AS PART OF A LARGER MEAL

12 to 16 ounces firm tofu

½ cup sliced yellow onion

¼ cup canola oil

3 cups finely diced yellow onion

2 tablespoons minced garlic

2 tablespoons minced ginger

1 to 3 Thai chiles, thinly sliced crosswise, or 3 tablespoons minced jalapeño

1 to 2 small dried chiles, broken in half, seeds retained

1¼ pounds kabocha squash (see page 33), peeled, seeded, and cut into 1-inch pieces (about 4 heaping cups)

½ teaspoon turmeric

¼ teaspoon paprika

2 teaspoons salt

½ teaspoon Tamarind Salt (page 217; optional)

2 cups water

½ teaspoon Garam Masala (page 216)

1 cup cilantro sprigs, for garnish

1 lime or lemon, cut into wedges, for garnish

Pork pairs well with something tart or sour to cut through its richness, which is how green mango comes into play. Made from tart unripe mangoes, Green Mango Pickle adds pucker power. You can make your own (see page 222) or buy a jar at a well-stocked grocery store or Indian market. There are about a million ways to go about making this pork curry, so vary as you wish. Add Thai chiles to amp up the spice. For a richer dish, add potatoes in the last half hour of cooking (like in the Beef Curry, page 37). And if sour is really your thing, add a few spoonfuls of Tamarind Water (page 218) at the end.

PORK CURRY
WITH GREEN MANGO PICKLE

SERVES 4; 6 AS PART OF A LARGER MEAL

2½ pounds boneless pork shoulder

1 tablespoon paprika

2 teaspoons turmeric

2 teaspoons salt

⅓ cup canola oil

1-ounce piece ginger, peeled and thickly sliced lengthwise into slabs

3 cups finely diced yellow onion

⅓ cup minced garlic

2 bay leaves

1 to 2 small dried chiles (optional)

2 tablespoons fish sauce

4 cups water

1 teaspoon Madras curry powder

½ teaspoon Garam Masala (page 216)

½ cup coarsely chopped Green Mango Pickle (page 222)

1 cup cilantro sprigs, for garnish

Tamarind Water, for garnish (optional; page 218)

Trim away the sinew from the pork, but leave some of the fat; it will add richness to the curry. Cut the pork into ½- to 1-inch pieces. Transfer to a bowl and use your hands to mix with the paprika, turmeric, and salt. Let the pork marinate at room temperature while you prepare the other ingredients, or refrigerate it overnight.

In a 6-quart pot, heat the oil over medium heat. Add the ginger and cook until the edges become lightly browned, 2 minutes. Add the onions and cook, stirring often to prevent scorching, until the onions have softened, about 4 minutes. Stir in the garlic, bay leaves, and chiles, decrease the heat to medium-low, and cook, stirring often, until most of the water from the onions has been cooked out and a glossy layer of oil has risen to the surface, about 10 minutes.

Add the pork and fish sauce and stir to coat. Pour in the water. Bring to a boil, then lower to a gentle simmer. Cook, stirring occasionally, until the meat is tender when pierced with a knife, about 1½ hours.

Stir in the curry powder, garam masala, and mango pickle. Pour in more water if the curry looks very thick. Cook over medium heat to combine the flavors, 10 to 15 minutes.

Ideally, let the curry sit for 20 minutes before serving to let the flavors meld. Bring to a simmer before serving and taste, adding more salt or fish sauce if desired. Serve with bowls of cilantro and tamarind water at the table.

While it's common for Burmese Buddhists to eat chicken and pork, many avoid beef—Desmond's mom, Eileen, has never once eaten it. Red meat in general can be hard to come by. In Myanmar, buffalo are needed to plow fields and few cattle farms exist in the country. When buying beef for this recipe, consider using grass-fed, which is more similar in taste and texture to the lean meat found in Myanmar. Or swap beef out entirely and make this recipe with lamb, which has an even deeper gamy quality that complements the spices. Lemongrass—common in meat curries from the Kayin people of Myanmar—helps temper any gamy aromas.

BEEF CURRY WITH POTATOES

SERVES 4; 6 AS PART OF A LARGAER MEAL

2½ pounds beef stew meat

1 tablespoon paprika

½ teaspoon turmeric

2 teaspoons salt

⅓ cup canola oil

1-ounce piece ginger, peeled and thickly sliced lengthwise into slabs

2 stalks lemongrass (see page 228), cut into 2-inch pieces

2½ cups finely diced yellow onion

⅓ cup minced garlic

2 to 3 thinly sliced Thai chiles or 2 small dried chiles

2 bay leaves

2 tablespoons fish sauce

Trim away the sinew from the beef and cut the meat into ½- to 1-inch cubes. Transfer to a bowl and use your hands to mix with the paprika, turmeric, and salt. Let the beef marinate at room temperature while you prepare the other ingredients, or refrigerate it overnight.

In a 6-quart pot, heat the oil over medium-high heat. Add the ginger and cook until the edges become lightly browned, 2 minutes. Stir in the lemongrass and cook until slightly softened, 2 minutes.

Add the onions, lower the heat to medium, and cook for 4 minutes, stirring often to keep the onions from sticking to the bottom of the pot. Stir in the garlic, chiles, and bay leaves. Decrease the heat to medium-low and cook, stirring often, until most of the water from the onions has been cooked out and a glossy layer of oil has risen to the surface, about 10 minutes.

Add the beef and fish sauce and stir to coat. Pour in the water. Increase the heat, bring to a boil, then lower to a gentle simmer. Cook, stirring occasionally, until the meat is beginning to become tender, about 1½ hours.

CONTINUED

Stir in the curry powder, garam masala, and potatoes. Pour in more water if the curry looks thick. Cook until the potatoes are tender, about 20 minutes more.

Ideally, let the curry sit for at least 20 minutes before serving to allow the beef to soak in the curry flavor as it cools. Bring to a simmer before serving, and taste, adding more salt or fish sauce if desired. Stir in the yogurt. Serve with bowls of cilantro and lime wedges at the table.

4 cups water

1 tablespoon Madras curry powder

¾ teaspoon Garam Masala (page 216)

1 pound Yukon gold potatoes (about 4), cubed

Spoonful of plain whole-milk or Greek yogurt (optional)

1 cup cilantro sprigs, for garnish

1 lime or lemon, cut into wedges, for garnish

VEGETABLES

You won't see the New Roots garden unless you know where to look—behind the bistro at Laney College in downtown Oakland.

There, gardeners tend beds of Chinese mustard greens, onions, pumpkin, chayote, chiles, garlic, chives, beans, and whatever else happens to be in season. In the summer, there could be fifty different plants growing, with cheery marigolds planted in between the rows. The 3,000-square-foot plot is productive. When one summer brought in a bumper crop of lemon cucumbers, a community-supported agriculture (CSA) program absorbed the extras.

Since 2013, the New Roots garden has been one of the International Rescue Committee's (IRC) initiatives to help refugees gain access to healthy, familiar food in their new environments. For many who grew up farming in rural communities in Asia, having access to a community garden makes them feel more at home. And the community gardens have been popular: the IRC now has New Roots programs in cities from New York to Seattle.

In Oakland, refugees from Myanmar, Bhutan, and Nepal share the garden, each ethnic group maintaining a section. Many live close enough to walk or take the bus to the campus. While some gardeners have specific preferences—the Bhutanese, for example, love nettles—there's a lot of produce crossover between the groups. Everyone eats Chinese mustard greens, and everyone has their own way of making pickles with them—which often requires drying the leaves in the sun beforehand. (Pickled mustard greens are a classic condiment with Shan Noodles, page 100.)

The garden also grows sour leaf—*chin baung* in Burmese—a favorite bitter green related to the hibiscus plant. It grows all over Myanmar, and Burmese immigrants in America quickly find their source. In refugee communities, those who grow it can make a good profit from selling it to other refugees. While the bulk of the sour leaf grown in the Oakland garden is taken home by the gardeners themselves, at the New Roots garden in Phoenix, sour leaf grows so well that gardeners can't cut it fast enough.

Many of the recipes in this chapter won't be found in the Burma Superstar restaurants, but they have been gathered from Burmese relatives and friends and during research trips to Myanmar. Serving one or two at the table with any of the curries, noodle dishes, or stir-fries in this book is the perfect way to make the book work for home-cooked meals. If you've never known what to do with chayote or water spinach, these simple sides will spark ideas. Having a pot of butter beans or spicy eggplant to eat alongside any salad, curry, or bowl of noodles goes a long way toward making a meal more complete. And you don't need a garden to gain access to the vegetables in this chapter. While cauliflower is available just about everywhere, water spinach, chayote, and pea shoots are easily found in Asian grocery stores, and at (often shockingly) good prices.

At traditional restaurants in Myanmar, every meal begins with a complimentary plate of raw vegetables paired with a pungent dipping sauce. It can be a brothy dip or a relish like this one, but it almost always contains shrimp paste and sometimes ground dried shrimp. Every cook has her own version, but the best of these condiments pack in an incredible amount of umami flavor. You can serve this as a dip with any assortment of crudités or go Burmese-style and eat it with tiny raw green eggplants, leafy bitter herbs, and half-moons of bitter melon. Instead of cleaning out the pot after making the relish, stir-fry day-old rice to soak up the flavor left behind. That's what one of Desmond's aunts likes to do.

TOMATO SHRIMP RELISH
WITH RAW VEGETABLES

MAKES ABOUT 3 CUPS RELISH; SERVES 10 AS AN APPETIZER

Relish

⅓ cup canola oil

----

3 cups finely diced yellow onion

¼ cup minced garlic

----

2 tablespoons shrimp paste (see page 238)

----

1 teaspoon paprika

----

1 teaspoon cayenne

¼ teaspoon turmeric

----

2 to 3 Thai chiles, thinly sliced crosswise

⅓ cup dried shrimp powder (see page 235)

----

5 cups diced Roma tomatoes (about 10 tomatoes)

In a 4-quart pot or deep saucepan, heat the oil over medium-high heat. Stir in the onions, decrease the heat to medium-low, and cook, stirring often, until the onions have browned around the edges and softened, 6 to 8 minutes.

Stir in the garlic and cook, stirring occasionally, until the garlic is very aromatic and the edges of the onions have started to brown, about 1 minute. Stir in the shrimp paste and cook for 1 minute.

Stir in the paprika, cayenne, turmeric, chiles, and shrimp powder and cook briefly. Stir in the tomatoes and bring to a simmer. Decrease the heat to low and cook, stirring often, until the water from the tomatoes has mostly evaporated and the relish has thickened, 10 to 15 minutes. The tomatoes will have turned from bright red to brick red.

Add 1 tablespoon fish sauce and the salt and cook for 1 minute more. Taste, adding 1 tablespoon or so of fish sauce (or a pinch of salt) for more impact. When the relish cools, a thin film of oil should rise to the surface.

CONTINUED

1 to 2 tablespoons fish sauce

1 teaspoon salt

**Crudités (any combination
of the following)**

1 to 2 cucumbers, sliced on an angle,
for dipping

¼ head cabbage, cut into thin wedges

Handful of cauliflower florets,
blanched

1 to 2 carrots, peeled and cut
into sticks

½ to 1 bitter melon, seeded and thinly
sliced (see sidebar)

Cilantro sprigs, for garnish

Bitter greens, such as sorrel leaves
or watercress

Before serving, give the relish a good stir. Transfer a cup or so to a bowl and serve with a platter of crudités. Garnish the top with cilantro sprigs. The rest of the relish will keep for 2 weeks in the refrigerator, although its color will brown a bit.

HOW TO PREPARE BITTER MELON

Like the other crunchy vegetables that come with the freebie relish plate at Burmese restaurants, bitter melon is a refreshing counterpoint to the rich relish. To prepare it, cut off the ends and slice it in half lengthwise. Scoop out any seeds or membranes and slice each half crosswise into half-moons. You can serve it as is or soak it in some water and a pinch of salt before serving to draw out some of the bitterness.

The best place to chill out after a hot day in Yangon is 19th Street, which becomes a small-scale version of a night market. Pick and choose what you want from various vendors cooking skewered fish, meat, and vegetables and then take a seat and order something to drink. Somehow, the vendors find you. Grilling vegetables, like okra, gives them a meaty, savory quality that perfectly complements Tomato Shrimp Relish. It all goes down easy with a chilled Myanmar beer.

GRILLED OKRA
WITH TOMATO SHRIMP RELISH

SERVES 4 AS A SIDE DISH

14 ounces okra (about 20), stem ends trimmed

1 tablespoon canola oil

Salt

1 cup Tomato Shrimp Relish (page 45), at room temperature

1 lime, cut into wedges

Preheat a grill over medium-high heat or have a grill pan ready. Soak wooden skewers if using a regular grill. If using a grill pan, you can skip the skewers.

In a bowl, mix together the okra, oil, and a couple of pinches of salt.

If using a regular grill, thread 4 or 5 okra onto each of 2 wooden skewers, keeping the skewers parallel to each other so the pods look like rungs on a ladder.

Grill the okra until nicely charred in parts, 3 to 4 minutes. Spread the relish across the bottom of a plate. Pull the okra off the skewers, if using, and scatter the okra over the relish. Serve with a bowl of lime wedges.

WHAT IS SOUR LEAF?

Sour leaf was nearly impossible to find in San Francisco a couple of decades ago. So when someone in the local Burmese community spotted the leafy green at a farmers' market, it was big news. But back in 2002, the supply was tight: Laotian farmers who grew it had only a limited amount because demand wasn't there. This changed quickly, especially as refugees from Myanmar began arriving in the Bay Area. By the mid-2000s, Burmese immigrants would buy whatever the farmers had— even placing orders in advance to secure supply for the following week.

Bite into sour leaf raw, and it tastes as described: sour. But start cooking with it and the initial bite turns to an easygoing sourness that actually improves when the leaf is cooked by the handful. Used to perk up soups and balance the flavors of bamboo and shrimp, sour leaf is a prized green in Myanmar. Related to hibiscus, sour leaf usually has a pointy three-prong leaf, but can also have a rounded leaf. Both are used in Myanmar, with the three-pronged leaf described as sour and the rounded leaf as bitter. When tasted alongside similarly strong-tasting french sorrel, sour leaf offers a more mellow, rounded flavor.

Nowadays, sour leaf supply is more dependable, but you still need to secure a source. More farmers specializing in Asian ingredients are aware of the value placed on sour leaf among Burmese, not only in California but also in Tennessee, North Carolina, Washington, Indiana, and other areas with growing Burmese communities. You still have to act fast. As soon as sour leaf appears before a farmers' market, word spreads in the Burmese community. While summer is the season for sour leaf in California, some years it's available as early as April. During the off-season, look for it in the frozen section of Asian groceries in areas with Burmese communities. (Kate found some in the back of a small grocery store specializing in Burmese ingredients in Greensboro, North Carolina.) Or make a Burmese friend and ask for a hookup.

Seemingly everyone who grew up in Myanmar loves *chin baung*, sour leaf, which grows all over the country. And everyone especially loves it with bamboo and shrimp, *chin baung kyaw*. This version of the recipe comes from Rahima, who is married to Har San, Burma Superstar's resident *platha* (flatbread) expert. The couple met in Chiang Mai, Thailand, but Rahima learned how to cook where she grew up—in a refugee camp on the border of Thailand and Burma. And even though her kids were born in America, Rahima says they prefer Burmese home cooking to American food. Bamboo is a classic match with sour leaf, the green's sourness offsetting bamboo's earthy flavors. Fresh bamboo shoots are not easy to find, but bamboo shoots vacuum-sealed in clear plastic packaging are available at many Asian markets. Look for them in the refrigerated sections. Preferable to canned, these bamboo shoots have already been peeled and poached, so all they need is a rinse before cooking.

SOUR LEAF
WITH BAMBOO AND SHRIMP

SERVES 4 TO 6 AS A SIDE DISH

2 cups coarsely chopped bamboo shoots

¼ cup canola oil

3 cups sliced yellow onion

2 tablespoons minced garlic

½ teaspoon turmeric

1 to 4 Thai chiles, halved lengthwise

2 teaspoons paprika

2 teaspoons salt

8 cups loosely packed fresh, stemmed sour leaf (about 2 bunches); or 2 cups frozen and thawed sour leaf; or 8 cups sorrel leaves

1 pound large shrimp (16–20 or 20–25 per pound), peeled and deveined

1 tablespoon fish sauce (optional)

Rinse the bamboo shoots and drain well.

In a 6-quart pot, heat the oil over medium heat. Add the onions, garlic, and chiles and cook for 4 minutes. Add the turmeric and paprika and cook for 1 minute more. Stir in the bamboo and the salt. Cook, stirring often, until the onions have softened, about 2 more minutes.

Add the sour leaf a couple handfuls at a time and cook, stirring to encourage the leaves to wilt, for 4 minutes more. Stir in the shrimp and cook until the shrimp is cooked through, about 2 minutes. The sour leaf will turn brown; that's okay. Taste, seasoning with fish sauce if desired.

The drive from Hsipaw to Namhsan in the Shan State is filled with cornfields. There are mixed opinions as to where all of this field corn is going—some say China; others say a Thai conglomerate. While none of this commodity product reaches Burmese tables, sweet corn is definitely eaten in Myanmar. What hits the table isn't as sweet as what we get in the States, and it varies in color too. Its preparations are kept simple. Some vendors sell corn on the cob steamed or roasted, while at home, many moms make this mild dish for their kids, the main flavor coming from sliced onions fried long enough to char a bit on the edges.

CORN WITH CHARRED ONIONS

SERVES 2 TO 4 AS A SIDE DISH

4 ears yellow corn

2 tablespoons plus 1 teaspoon canola oil

1 cup sliced yellow onion or shallot

½ teaspoon salt

¼ teaspoon dried chile flakes

Shuck the corn and wipe off the corn silk. Stand the cob upright on a cutting board. Angling the knife downward and slightly inward, cut the kernels off the cob. You should have about 4 cups.

In a wok or pot with a lid, heat the 2 tablespoons of oil over medium-high heat. Add the onions and cook, lowering the heat to medium and stirring often, until the onions are golden brown and charred around the edges, 8 to 10 minutes. Using a slotted spoon, transfer the onions to a plate.

Add the remaining 1 teaspoon oil to the wok and heat over medium-high heat. Add the corn and cook, stirring occasionally, until the kernels begin to char and pop like popcorn (if they start going crazy, use the lid to partially cover the wok). Stir-fry until the corn is cooked but not mushy, about 2 minutes. Season with salt and chile flakes and stir in the onions to serve.

Chayote (*chai-OH-tee*) is a light green fruit about the size of a quince or pear, with a dense texture and mild flavor. While technically a fruit, it's cooked like a vegetable. (Its greens are used in stir-fries too.) This simple Chinese-style side dish was one of Desmond's favorites growing up. To prepare chayote, peel away the tough green skin before slicing. If you have trouble finding chayote, use 4 cups sliced green cabbage in its place. Look for chayote in Asian and Latin American grocery stores.

Peel the chayotes and quarter lengthwise. Slice crosswise into thin ¼-inch-thick slabs.

Put the shrimp in a bowl and cover with hot water. Soak for 10 minutes. Drain and squeeze the excess water out of the shrimp.

In a large, heavy pot, heat the oil over medium heat. Add the garlic and cook briefly, about 10 seconds. Stir in the chayote, shrimp, and salt. Continue to cook, stirring, for 2 minutes, until the chayote barely begins to brown on the edges. Add a splash of water and cook until softened, about 2 minutes more.

Stir in the peanut oil and pepper. Taste, adding more salt or pepper if desired.

CHAYOTE WITH DRIED SHRIMP

SERVES 2 TO 4 AS A SIDE DISH

2 chayotes (about 1 pound)

¼ cup dried shrimp (see page 235)

1 tablespoon canola oil

1 tablespoon minced garlic

¾ teaspoon salt

1 teaspoon peanut oil or sesame oil (optional)

¼ teaspoon ground white or black pepper

At the Burma Superstar wok station, broccoli is briefly blanched, drip-dried, and then stir-fried quickly in a powerful wok to get that addictive bit of char on the florets. This version has been modified slightly assuming your home does not have access to the same number of BTUs. To make the most of a head of broccoli, use the stalks too. Peel away the tough skin and slice the stalks into coins. Or go with broccoli's skinny cousin, broccolini, which cooks much faster. Slice the broccolini stems into pieces about 2 inches long and keep the small florets intact.

WOK-TOSSED BROCCOLI

SERVES 4 AS A SIDE DISH

2 tablespoons canola oil

2 garlic cloves, thinly sliced

8 ounces small broccoli florets and stalks (about 4 cups)

1 small dried chile, broken in half, or a pinch of dried chile flakes

1 tablespoon rice wine (optional)

½ teaspoon salt

In a large wok or pot, heat the oil over medium heat. Swirl the oil in the wok and add the garlic. Stir-fry until lightly golden and fragrant, about 20 seconds. Turn off the heat, use a slotted spoon to remove the garlic from the wok, and set the garlic aside. Leave the oil in the wok.

Heat the wok over high heat and add the broccoli and chile. Stir-fry until some of the florets have a little char on them, about 1 minute. Add the wine, salt, and a spoonful of water and continue to cook until the broccoli has softened but is still crisp, about 2 minutes more. Return the garlic to the wok and toss to coat.

Chinese-style stir-fried pea shoots are a refreshing side dish for any meal of slow-cooked curry and rich noodles. Before you start stir-frying, cut the pea shoots into 2- to 3-inch pieces. (Bags of pre-cut pea shoots are often available at Asian markets.) To help them steam a bit in the wok, leave a little water clinging to the leaves after washing them.

WOK-TOSSED PEA SHOOTS

In a large wok or pot, heat the oil over medium heat. Swirl the oil in the wok and add the garlic. Stir-fry until lightly golden and fragrant, about 20 seconds. Turn off the heat, use a slotted spoon to remove the garlic from the wok, and set the garlic aside. Leave the oil in the wok.

Heat the wok over high heat and add the pea shoots, chile, and wine. Stir-fry, stirring constantly, until the leaves have wilted but the stems are still crisp, about 1 minute. Return the garlic to the wok and toss to coat. Season with salt.

SERVES 2 TO 4 AS A SIDE DISH

2 tablespoons canola oil

----

3 garlic cloves, thinly sliced

----

8 ounces pea shoots
(about 8 packed cups)

----

1 small dried chile, broken in half,
or a pinch of dried chile flakes

----

1 tablespoon rice wine (optional)

½ teaspoon salt

Grown all over Southeast Asia, water spinach has a million names. It can be called morning glory, Hong Kong spinach, or ong choy. During the monsoon season in Myanmar, water spinach is a regular part of the vegetable rotation. It's widely popular for a reason: its tender spinach-like leaves and hollow stems readily soak up flavor.

There are two kinds of water spinach. One has long, skinny leaves while the other has wider, heart-shaped leaves (pictured). Both have the plant's signature hollow stems and can be prepared the same way. Look for the vegetable in bags at Chinese grocery stores. While the stems of the water spinach pictured here is on the short side, water spinach can grow quite long. If the stems are long, you may have more stems than greens, but that's perfectly fine. For a vegetarian version, omit the shrimp paste and 1 tablespoon of soy sauce.

WATER SPINACH

SERVES 2 TO 4 AS A SIDE DISH

12 ounces water spinach, about 10 cups

1 tablespoon canola oil

2 garlic cloves, thinly sliced

½ Thai chile, thinly sliced crosswise, or 1 tablespoon minced jalapeño

2 teaspoons shrimp paste (see page 238)

Pinch of salt

Line a baking sheet with a kitchen towel and fill a large bowl with water.

Twist off the base of the water spinach bunches. Using your hands or scissors, separate the thicker stems from the tender tops. (The ends take longer to cook, so you'll add those to the wok first.) Using scissors or a knife, trim the hollow stems into pieces about 3 inches long. The leafy tops can be longer.

Submerge the leaves in the bowl of water and give them a good wash, then spread them out on one side of the kitchen towel to drain. Repeat with the stems, spreading them on the other side of the towel.

In a wok or large pot, heat the oil over medium heat. Swirl the oil in the wok and add the garlic, chile, and shrimp paste. Stir-fry until the garlic begins to brown, about 15 seconds. Add the spinach stems, decrease the heat to medium-low, and cook until the stems start to soften, about 1 minute. (Don't worry if the stems are still wet; the water clinging to the stems will keep the garlic from burning.)

Stir in the leaves, partially cover the wok, and cook until the spinach leaves have wilted, 1 to 2 minutes. If the wok is dry and the leaves start to stick, add a spoonful of water. Taste, seasoning with salt if desired, and stir-fry for 1 minute more or until the leaves are tender but the stems are still a bit crunchy.

Cauliflower is grown in the Shan hills, where it's packed into trucks or onto trains destined for Mandalay and Yangon. We came across this simple dish of sautéed cauliflower and tomato while visiting the temple town of Bagan. There, a beaten egg was poured over the top and stirred in at the end to give it richness, but the vegetables stand alone just fine without the egg. When re-creating it in California, we found that tamarind salt made a nice addition to the vegetables. For a spicier, even saltier take, drizzle soy sauce over the veggies and finish with a heaping spoonful of *sambal oelek* (see page 238).

CAULIFLOWER AND TOMATO

SERVES 3 TO 4 AS A SIDE DISH

1 pound cauliflower florets (about 4 heaping cups)

¼ cup canola oil

½ teaspoon salt

2 large shallots or ¼ red onion, sliced

2 Roma tomatoes, sliced thinly lengthwise

1 teaspoon Tamarind Salt (page 217; optional)

1 cup cilantro sprigs, coarsely chopped

1 lime or lemon, cut into wedges

Give the cauliflower a once-over, slicing any of the larger florets in half or in quarters to ensure even cooking.

In a wok or pot with a lid, heat the oil over medium-high heat. Add the cauliflower and the salt. Cover, decrease the heat to low, and cook 4 minutes or until the cauliflower starts to brown and soften.

Uncover and add the shallots. Continue to cook stirring often, until the shallots begin to soften, 2 minutes. Add the tomatoes, increase the heat to medium-high, and cook until the tomatoes begin to break down, the cauliflower is cooked through, and most of the water has evaporated, about 1 minute more.

Taste, seasoning with tamarind salt or regular salt as needed. Sprinkle cilantro over the top. Serve with a bowl of lime wedges at the table.

When traveling through central Myanmar during the dry season, a side of pale yellow beans is a staple. A couple of days ahead, cooks soak, strain, and then cover the beans to encourage them to sprout, making them easier to digest. This recipe modifies the process a bit, using easy-to-find dried lima beans and skipping the sprouting step. The rest of the dish is just as no-fuss, but if you want to dress it up, sprinkle some Fried Onions (page 208) on top when serving. Serve the beans alongside Pork Curry with Green Mango Pickle (page 36), Pumpkin Pork Stew (page 33), or any of the kebats (starting on page 81).

BAGAN BUTTER BEANS

MAKES ABOUT 3 CUPS; SERVES 4 AS A SIDE DISH

2 cups dried lima beans

2 teaspoons salt

2 tablespoons canola oil

2 cups diced yellow onion or shallot

Heaping ¼ teaspoon turmeric

Rinse the beans well in a colander, picking out any pebbles. Put the beans in a bowl and cover with 2 inches of cool water. Let soak for at least 4 hours or overnight.

Drain the beans and transfer to a 4-quart pot. Add water to cover by 2 inches. Place over high heat and bring to a boil, stirring occasionally to prevent any foam from boiling over. Lower the heat to a gentle simmer and cook uncovered until tender, about 1 hour. Remove the beans from the heat, stir in the salt, and let the beans stand in their cooking water for at least 30 minutes. This will allow them to absorb the salt. At this point, you can refrigerate the beans and finish the recipe the next day.

Drain the beans, reserving the bean cooking water. Give the pot a quick rinse, dry it, and then heat it over medium-high heat. Pour in the oil and add the onions. Lower the heat to medium and cook until the onions have softened and are starting to brown, about 5 minutes. Add the turmeric and cook for 1 minute more. Stir in the beans and about 1 cup of the reserved bean cooking water and simmer gently until the beans have thickened, about 5 minutes more. The beans may fall apart as they cook, but this is perfectly okay. Taste, seasoning with more salt if desired.

PA-O BEANS

While we were researching Burmese food for this book, cookbook author Andrea Nguyen put Kate in touch with journalist Karen Coates. Karen, along with her husband, photojournalist Jerry Redfern, have extensive experience reporting (and eating) throughout Southeast Asia, including in Myanmar. One of the Burmese dishes Karen recounted was something she sampled while trekking across the Shan State in 2002 with Jerry. It was a humble pot of beans made by a Pa-O family, one of Myanmar's many minority groups.

But it was the way the beans were infused with garlic, ginger, and peanut oil that made them memorable enough for Karen to recreate the dish at home in New Mexico. To create a similar version of Karen's Pa-O beans, modify the Bagan Butter Beans (see opposite page) by adding five smashed garlic cloves and a tablespoon or so of minced ginger to the pot once the onion starts to soften. Before serving, drizzle an aromatic peanut oil over the beans and sprinkle sliced green onions on top.

Serve this curry-style eggplant as a side dish or, paired with the Ginger Salad (page 128), as a main course. In Myanmar, tiny green eggplants are liked so much that they're even served raw (but make no mistake: they are still truly bitter). For this version, opt for slender Japanese or Chinese eggplants. To make it vegetarian, leave out the shrimp paste and fish sauce and season with Tamarind Salt (page 217). This curry packs some heat. To tone down the spice level, opt for jalapeño over Thai chile.

SPICY EGGPLANT

SERVES 3 TO 4 AS A SIDE DISH

3 Japanese eggplants, cut into 1-inch cubes (about 6 cups)

1 teaspoon salt

2½ tablespoons canola oil

2 cups finely diced yellow onion

3 tablespoons minced garlic

1 tablespoon minced ginger

1 to 2 Thai chiles, thinly sliced, or 2 tablespoons minced jalapeño

1 small dried chile, broken in half, seeds retained (optional)

2 teaspoons shrimp paste (see page 238)

½ teaspoon turmeric

½ teaspoon paprika

1 teaspoon fish sauce

Handful of Fried Garlic Chips (page 211; optional)

Cilantro sprigs, for garnish

1 lime or lemon, cut into wedges, for garnish

Season the eggplant with salt and scatter onto a clean dish towel. Let it sit while you prepare the remaining ingredients, at least 10 minutes. Once the eggplant begins to bead with water, wrap the towel tightly and squeeze to remove excess liquid from the eggplant.

In a wok or pot, heat 1 tablespoon of the oil over medium-high heat. Add the eggplant, lower the heat to medium, and cook, stirring often, until the eggplant begins to soften, about 4 minutes. Using a slotted spoon, scoop out the eggplant and transfer to a plate.

Heat the remaining 1½ tablespoons of oil in the wok. Add the onions and cook over medium-low heat, stirring often to prevent scorching, until softened, about 4 minutes. Stir in the garlic, ginger, fresh and dried chiles, and shrimp paste and cook until the onions are completely soft and starting to turn golden, 3 more minutes.

Add the turmeric and paprika and then stir in the eggplant and about ½ cup of water. Lower to a gentle simmer and cook, stirring occasionally, until the eggplant is very soft and most of the water has evaporated, about 5 minutes. Season with fish sauce, adding more for a saltier flavor, and squeeze a wedge or two of lime over the top.

Serve in a bowl and top with cilantro. Offer extra lime wedges alongside.

A BID FOR DEMOCRACY

From 1962—when a military junta took control from a struggling civilian government—until the reforms that began in 2011 and 2012, Myanmar was a country cut off from the rest of the world. For half a century, the government controlled businesses, censored the press, and limited contact with the outside world.

On Sunday, November 8, 2015, Myanmar turned a corner. Facebook posts began filling with photos documenting the lines forming outside polling stations to vote in the country's general election. The streets were quiet. A trip from uptown to downtown that would usually take an hour in traffic lasted only fifteen minutes. Many citizens were casting votes for the first time in a free and fair election, an act that would have seemed impossible a decade earlier. By Monday afternoon, crowds were cheering, holding NLD (National League for Democracy) banners, and celebrating their party's victory.

"The days after the election were surreal," said Sarah Oh, an American living in Yangon who had been working with voter groups on ways to use technology to help spread election information. "No one was sure what would happen next. Now, looking back, it was clear that there was a new confidence and feeling in the air. People felt like individuals could finally make a difference or have a say."

The party in power, the Union Solidarity and Development Party led by President Thein Sein, a former general, lost by a landslide to the NLD. The NLD was a party headed by Nobel laureate and former political prisoner Aung San Suu Kyi, a woman who had spent fifteen years under house arrest. In 1990, the last time her party won an election, the government had ignored the results.

Change had already begun a few years before the historic election; Myanmar had started to become a different place. Beginning in 2011, the military started to loosen up, putting a nominally civilian government in power. President Sein became the first Burmese president to visit the United States in forty-eight years. He also started releasing political prisoners and ended media censorship. Meanwhile, the United States and other countries began lifting some trade sanctions, and private companies—and money—began flowing into Yangon. By 2015, the price of office space in Yangon rivaled that of New York and Singapore. The cost of cars, while still prohibitively high for most Burmese, also began to drop, and traffic began to resemble the gridlock in cities like Bangkok.

The cost of staying connected within the country also decreased—significantly. Buying a SIM card for a mobile phone dropped from $2,000 in 2009 to about $1.50 in 2014, reported journalists Karen Coates and Jerry Redfern on SciDev.net. A country that never had reliable phone service was now inundated with mobile phones. And seemingly everyone with access to the Internet joined Facebook.

At Sharky's, a restaurant in an affluent neighborhood of Yangon, tables are always packed with foreigners craving European food: caprese salad

made with buffalo milk mozzarella, steak, and wood-fired pizza. U Ye Htut Hin—who calls himself Sharky—got his start in the restaurant business at a Wendy's in Switzerland. He grows or makes more than eighty percent of what he serves, including microgreens, artisan breads and cheeses, and sea salt harvested from Myanmar's coast. Most of the time, growing and making these things himself is the only way to guarantee the supply of these luxuries. Since foreign business started taking an interest in the city, the demand for Sharky's restaurant and retail products had become so strong that a few months before the election, Sharky and his business partner, Jane Brooks, opened a second space downtown. Jane told us that no matter what happens politically, it's unlikely that the momentum of foreign-business growth in Yangon will stop. The hope is that these business interests will also keep the government moving in a progressive direction.

The results of the election haven't been perfect. Although her party won, Daw Suu ("Aunt Suu," the polite Burmese way to refer to Aung San Suu Kyi) cannot become president because the constitution forbids anyone who has foreign relatives from holding office. (Her two sons are half British.) So Htin Kyaw, a prodemocracy advocate and son of a renowned poet, became president on Daw Suu's behalf. He is the first civilian president in fifty-four years. Meanwhile, conflict between the military and ethnic rebel groups in the Shan, Kachin, and Chin states continues. At the writing of this book, Rohingya Muslims in Rakhine State were living in legal limbo, not accepted by the Burmese as citizens.

There are also plenty of remnants from the previous regime. In 2005, the government moved the capital from Yangon to a place they eventually named Nay Pyi Taw, a new city built amid fields of commodity crops between Yangon and Mandalay—the cultural equivalent of the middle of nowhere. More than a decade later, its empty boulevards are baffling sites compared to the packed streets of Yangon and Mandalay. While Nay Pyi Taw has new roads, the rest of the country's infrastructure has been neglected, from unpaved roads to bumpy train lines built during the British colonial days. Many rural areas don't have electricity. Even in Yangon, public utilities can't be relied upon. To keep business humming, Sharky's has full-time electricians on staff and maintains its own water filtration system.

By the time this book is printed, it will still be too early to determine what the lasting effects of the November 2015 election will be. Yet compared to 1990, when the election results quickly became meaningless, this has been an enormous step forward. For the first time in decades, the people of Myanmar—whether they live here or there—have reason to believe that their country is heading toward a better future.

STIR-FRIES AND FAST-COOKED DISHES

Wai K. Law—known to everyone at the
Clement Street location as Jacky Chan—grew up in
Guangzhou, China, where he attended a cooking school
in which Chinese techniques—knife cuts,
stir-frying, steaming—were drilled into students.

After arriving in San Francisco in 1994, Jacky was juggling two restaurant jobs when he met the Wus, Burma Superstar's first owners. Jacky, who has a slight build and quick wit, impressed the Wus, who hired him to work the wok station. Though the menu has shrunk since Jacky's first day, he can still cook all the old dishes that are no longer listed: Singapore noodles? Easy. Just chile, and some curry powder. Why do you need a recipe? And nobody, insists the Clement Street staff, makes better steamed eggs.

Chinese stir-frying uses firepower more than any other kind of stove-top cooking method, and as a consequence, it's not easy to teach someone in words, Jacky says. A cook must learn through experience.

At Oakland's Burma Superstar, Mr. Ma echoes the importance of putting in time. Born in Taiwan, he grew up learning how to cook in his family's restaurant before moving to America in the 1980s. When Desmond was putting together an opening crew in Oakland, Mr. Ma was looking for a new job. Desmond hired Mr. Ma a week before the Oakland restaurant opened.

When the restaurant gets busy—which is consistently from 5:00 to 10:00 p.m.—Mr. Ma goes to battle against the deluge of orders, pouring oil into the wok, stir-frying protein and vegetables, and spooning food onto plates. Every fluid movement conserves energy. The station gets slammed in a way that would rattle a less experienced cook, but Mr. Ma just shrugs: the busier it gets, the better he works. "Old soldiers never die," he says, partially borrowing a quote from General MacArthur.

When it comes to how well Chinese stir-fry melds with Burmese cooking, Chuck Chin doesn't think the two are at odds with each other. Chuck was born in Yangon and later moved to Houston and then to Oakland. He spent years cooking in Chinese restaurants and airline commissary kitchens before landing at the Alameda Burma Superstar, where he is in charge of the Chinese side of the menu. Chinese food in Yangon is less sweet and spicier than American-style Chinese, he says.

Since these recipes have been written with a home kitchen in mind, they have been modified to ensure that those of us without restaurant-strength wok stations can make perfectly flavorful renditions of fast-cooked dishes. For instance, instead of adding flavoring sauces directly into the wok, as they do in the restaurants, these recipes instruct you to mix sauces together ahead of time. This allows you to keep the focus on cooking—not measuring—when you're in the heat of the moment.

To make Fiery Tofu, Mr. Ma fries the green beans, tofu, and bell pepper together until the green beans are cooked through and slightly blistered. Then he drains the oil out of the wok before he stir-fries the aromatics. This dry-frying Chinese cooking method, in which food is fried, drained of oil, and then stir-fried with seasoning, gives the tofu and vegetables the perfect texture to carry the spicy sauce. To make this preparation more home-kitchen friendly, we reduced the oil to allow us to skip the oil-draining step. To ensure the green beans are adequately fried, tilt the wok so that the oil pools to one side.

For this dish, look for extra-firm or super-firm tofu, which is denser and drier than firm tofu and hold their shape much better in stir-fries. Tofu labeled "braised" or "baked," which is essentially super-firm tofu cooked with seasoning can also be used in this recipe. You can use meat in place of the tofu; first stir-fry the meat and then set it aside. Return it to the wok after stir-frying the garlic and ginger. For a vegetarian version of fiery tofu, omit the oyster sauce.

FIERY TOFU

In a bowl, whisk together the sambal, soy sauces, oyster sauce, vinegar, and sugar.

In a wok or large skillet, heat the oil over medium heat. Add the green beans and cook, tilting the wok so the oil coats the beans, until the beans begin to blister, about 1 minute. Add the tofu and bell pepper and fry until the beans begin to wrinkle, about 2 minutes. Using a slotted spoon, transfer the tofu and vegetables to a plate, leaving oil in the wok.

Add the garlic and ginger to the wok and stir-fry briefly, about 20 seconds. Return the tofu and vegetables to the wok and pour in the sambal mixture. Cook for a minute or so until the tofu is nicely coated in the sauce. Stir in the basil and serve immediately.

SERVES 2; 4 AS PART OF A LARGER MEAL

1½ tablespoons sambal oelek (see page 238)

1 tablespoon soy sauce

1½ teaspoons dark soy sauce

1½ teaspoons oyster sauce

1 teaspoon distilled white vinegar

1 teaspoon sugar

2 tablespoons canola oil

1 cup green beans, ends trimmed

8 to 10 ounces super-firm tofu, sliced into bite-sized strips

1 red bell pepper, seeded and sliced into thin strips

1 tablespoon minced garlic

1 tablespoon minced ginger

Handful of Thai basil leaves

The star of this dish is a rich paste made by gently cooking garlic in oil. The recipe yields twice as much paste as is needed, so you can make the paste once and use it to make the recipe twice, with a little left over for stir-frying rice or seasoning noodles. The garlic paste also makes this stir-fry recipe foolproof (no need to worry about burning the garlic while you cook the shrimp). To make peeling the garlic easier, break up the heads and soak the cloves in water for a few minutes beforehand.

GARLIC CHILE SHRIMP

SERVES 3; 4 AS PART OF A LARGER MEAL

Garlic Paste

2 heads garlic, broken into cloves and peeled

½ cup canola oil

1 teaspoon paprika

¼ teaspoon turmeric

1 tablespoon fish sauce

Salt (optional)

Garlic Chile Shrimp

¼ cup garlic paste

1 pound large shrimp (16–20 or 20–25 per pound), peeled and deveined

½ cup sliced yellow onion or shallot

1 small dried chile, broken in half, seeds retained

½ jalapeño, sliced crosswise

Salt (optional)

Cilantro sprigs, for garnish

To make the garlic paste, put the garlic cloves in a small saucepan. If any are much larger than the others, cut them in half so they cook more evenly. Cover with the oil and place over low heat. Cook at a lazy simmer, stirring occasionally, until the garlic cloves have softened and turned from white to golden but aren't falling apart, about 15 minutes. Watch the garlic carefully: you should see small bubbles forming along the sides of the cloves. The oil should not be bubbling vigorously. Remove the pan from the heat and let the garlic cool in the oil to warm room temperature.

In a food processor, puree the garlic and oil with the paprika and turmeric. Blend in the fish sauce and taste, adding more fish sauce or a pinch of salt if the paste isn't noticeably salty. (It will be where the shrimp get most of their flavor, so it should be assertive.) You will have about ½ cup of paste, twice what you need for one recipe of garlic chile shrimp. The extra can be refrigerated and keeps for at least 3 months.

To make the garlic chile shrimp, mix the garlic paste into the shrimp in a bowl. Heat a wok or large skillet over high heat. Add the shrimp and stir-fry, letting the shrimp sear against the base of the wok (by avoiding constant stirring) for 2 minutes. Add the onions, chile, and jalapeño and cook until the onion has softened but is still slightly crisp and the shrimp is cooked through, about 1 minute more. Taste, adding salt as desired. Sprinkle cilantro on top before serving.

Those who like *laap* will love this Burmese-Chinese version of the herby Thai minced meat dish. Here, minced chicken is stir-fried with ground cumin and mustard seeds, ginger, garlic, and a spoonful of *sambal oelek* (see page 238). Whole cloves of garlic are mixed in for texture, but they are fried ahead of time to reduce the pungency of eating them raw. Use the smaller cloves found on the inside of a head of garlic or slice large cloves in half. You can turn this into a vegetarian dish by dicing up a block of firm tofu, letting it drain on paper towels for a few minutes, and then stir-frying the tofu pieces in place of the chicken. If you made the Mustard-Cumin Spice Blend (see page 215), use a teaspoon of it in place of the mustard and cumin seeds called for below.

To mince the chicken, place the pieces on the cutting board so the smooth side is facing up. With a knife blade parallel to the cutting board, slice the chicken in half width-wise, opening it up into two thinner, even pieces. Cut the chicken against the grain into thin strips, then chop the strips finely. Run the knife over the meat until it looks evenly minced. (Cutting the chicken by hand results in a better texture than using ground chicken.)

In a dry wok or skillet, toast the cumin seeds and mustard seeds until the cumin is fragrant and the mustard seeds start to pop, no more than 30 seconds. Transfer to a mortar with a pestle or a coffee grinder used for grinding spices and pulverize into a coarse powder.

In a small bowl, mix together the sambal, soy sauce, fish sauce, and sugar. (If not using soy sauce, you may need a pinch more fish sauce.)

In a wok or large skillet, heat the oil over medium heat. Tilt the wok so the oil pools to one side and add the garlic cloves. (This helps the garlic cloves stay submerged in oil so they fry more evenly.) Fry until light golden and softened, about 1 minute. Use a slotted spoon to remove the garlic cloves. Leave the oil in the wok.

Heat the wok over high heat. When the oil is hot (but not smoking), add the minced garlic and ginger. Stir-fry for a few seconds and add the chicken. Using a spatula or wooden spoon, stir-fry the chicken briefly, then press the meat against the sides of the wok to increase

CONTINUED

CHICKEN WITH MINT

SERVES 3; 4 AS PART OF A LARGER MEAL

1 pound boneless, skinless chicken breasts (about 2 small) or 4 to 5 boneless, skinless chicken thighs

½ teaspoon cumin seeds

½ teaspoon black mustard seeds

2 tablespoons sambal oelek (see page 238)

1 tablespoon dark soy sauce or 1 teaspoon salt

1 teaspoon fish sauce

¼ teaspoon sugar

2 tablespoons canola oil

6 to 8 small garlic cloves

1 teaspoon minced garlic

1 teaspoon minced ginger

½ jalapeño, chopped, or 2 Thai chiles, sliced

¼ cup chopped cilantro, plus extra sprigs for garnish

¼ cup chopped mint

Lime wedges, for garnish

the surface area and decrease how much the chicken steams. (If using a skillet, spread the chicken evenly across its base.) Water will start to pool in the center of the wok, but that's okay—it will cook out. After a minute, give the wok a stir so the chicken pieces don't stick together. Repeat this step until the chicken is light brown in places and pale in others, about 3 minutes depending on the wok and the burner strength.

Stir in the mustard-cumin blend, sambal mixture, fried garlic cloves, and jalapeño. Stir constantly, until the liquid just lightly coats the meat. Mix in the chopped cilantro and mint. Serve with cilantro sprigs and lime wedges.

This stir-fry is a Pan-Asian bonanza of textures and flavors. Chicken is sliced into strips and stir-fried with minced lemongrass, snow peas, and bell pepper, and everything is finished with a handful of Thai basil. The key to achieving the dark color and savory flavor is to use a combination of light (regular) and dark soy sauce (see page 238).

CHICKEN WITH BASIL

SERVES 3; 4 AS PART OF A LARGER MEAL

1 tablespoon sambal oelek (see page 238)

1½ teaspoons soy sauce

1½ teaspoons dark soy sauce

1 teaspoon cornstarch

½ teaspoon sugar

1 tablespoon water

2 tablespoons canola oil

1 tablespoon minced lemongrass (see page 228; optional)

2 tablespoons minced garlic

1 pound boneless, skinless chicken breasts (about 2 small), sliced crosswise into thin strips

½ red bell pepper, seeded and sliced into thin strips

4 ounces snow peas, trimmed and halved on a diagonal (about 1 heaping cup)

Dried chile flakes (optional)

Salt (optional)

½ cup loosely packed Thai basil leaves, for garnish

1 lime or lemon, cut into wedges, for garnish

In a small bowl, mix together the sambal, soy sauces, cornstarch, sugar, and water.

Heat a wok or large skillet over high heat. Add 1 tablespoon of the oil and swirl to coat the sides. Add the chicken and stir-fry until the pieces have separated and are lightly browned and nearly cooked, about 2 minutes. Transfer to a plate.

Wipe out the wok and heat the remaining 1 tablespoon of oil over medium-high heat. Add the garlic and lemongrass, and cook, stirring constantly with a wok spatula or wooden spoon, until the garlic is aromatic, about 15 seconds. Add the bell pepper and snow peas and cook for 30 more seconds.

Add the chicken and the sambal mixture and continue to cook, stirring constantly, until the liquid lightly coats the meat and the meat is cooked through. Season with a couple of pinches of chile flakes and salt. Sprinkle the basil leaves on top. Serve lime wedges alongside.

On the Burma Superstar menu, sesame chicken has been a crowd favorite going back decades. Kids get hooked on its sweet flavor (the sauce includes honey), and the addiction lasts into adulthood. "American people like things more sweet," says Chuck Chin, the lead Chinese cook at the Alameda location. If a group of people can't agree on what to eat, sesame chicken is a reliable way to go. It's also a popular lunch plate with jasmine rice and ginger salad. This version skips the deep-frying step in favor of a modified shallow-frying technique.

SESAME CHICKEN

Combine the chicken, the cornstarch, salt, and pepper in a bowl and let sit at room temperature while you prepare the remaining ingredients.

In a bowl, whisk together the vinegar, soy sauces, honey, sugar, and water.

Have a bowl, a slotted spoon, and a heat-proof vessel for storing hot oil handy. In a wok or large skillet, heat the oil over medium heat for about 1 minute. Add one piece of chicken to test the heat of the oil—if bubbles form rapidly around the chicken, the oil is ready. In two batches, fry the chicken until it is nearly cooked through, about 1½ minutes. Using a slotted spoon, transfer to the bowl. Repeat with the remaining chicken. Pour off the oil.

Add the sauce to the wok and cook briefly until nearly boiling, about 1 minute. Return the chicken to the wok and cook over medium heat until the sauce coats the chicken and the chicken is cooked through, 1 to 2 more minutes. Sprinkle sesame seeds and green onions on top, toss to coat, and serve.

SERVES 3; 4 AS PART OF A LARGER MEAL

1 pound boneless, skinless chicken breasts (about 2 small), sliced crosswise into thin, bite-sized strips

3 tablespoons cornstarch

1 teaspoon salt

½ teaspoon ground pepper

2 tablespoons distilled white vinegar

1 tablespoon soy sauce

1 teaspoon dark soy sauce

1 tablespoon honey

½ teaspoon sugar (optional)

¼ cup water

½ cup canola oil

2 tablespoons toasted sesame seeds

2 green onions, thinly sliced

KEBAT: HOME-STYLE AND RESTAURANT-STYLE

Burma Superstar's menu has four kinds of kebat: chicken, shrimp, tofu, and beef. While this stir-fried dish is a key item at the restaurant, it is nearly impossible to find on restaurant menus in Myanmar—and we looked. But Khin Ye' Yupar Aye, whose husband's family owns Shan Shwe Taung, a *laphet* (fermented tea leaf) company based in Mandalay, confirmed that it's a pretty common preparation. "Kebat? Yes, I know kebat," she said. It's something she ate at home while growing up in Yangon.

A product of Myanmar's cultural melting pot, kebat is best known by residents of Yangon and Mandalay as a home-cooked dish that likely evolved from skewered meats grilled in street-side food stalls in Muslim neighborhoods. Somewhere along the way, it lost the skewers, making it an even easier dish to cook at home with a few spices. Desmond's mom, Eileen, says first you marinate the protein in a little curry powder and fish sauce while preparing the onions and garlic. Then you start cooking the minced onions before adding the garlic to allow some of the water in the onions to evaporate. When you add the sliced onions at the end, don't cook them too long or the onions will get soft. If using fish or shrimp instead of chicken, add ginger and shrimp paste. And that's it.

Yet while kebat remained a simple home-cooked dish in Myanmar, it morphed into a restaurant-style stir-fry in California. The restaurant version uses more spices and offers a version with tofu. While homemade kebat can be prepared in either a wok, skillet, or pot over medium heat, restaurant-style kebat is always prepared in a sizzling wok.

Because these two styles are very different from each other, we have included four recipes, two representing homemade versions and two derived from restaurant-style versions. The latter, requires a spice mix, which is listed below.

Kebat Spice Mix

3 green cardamom pods

¼ teaspoon cumin seeds

1½ teaspoons salt

½ teaspoon paprika

½ teaspoon ground black pepper

¼ teaspoon cayenne

¼ teaspoon turmeric

¼ teaspoon cinnamon

¼ teaspoon sugar

To make the spice blend, crush the cardamom pods to open them up, then remove the seeds and discard the pods. Put the cardamom seeds and cumin seeds in a mortar with a pestle or a coffee grinder used for grinding spices and pulverize to a coarse powder. Add the salt and remaining ingredients and blend together.

The spices in this version of kebat give the tofu a rich toasted flavor that makes this vegetarian dish something that satisfies even the most meat-loving eaters. To boost the vegetable content, add any vegetables you happen to have on hand, from sliced bell peppers to snap peas to even chayote, when you add the onions, garlic, ginger, and jalapeño. For notes about super-firm tofu, see Fiery Tofu (page 73).

RESTAURANT-STYLE TOFU KEBAT

SERVES 3; 4 AS PART OF A LARGER MEAL

10 ounces super-firm tofu, cut into bite-sized strips

Kebat Spice Mix (see page 81)

2 tablespoons canola oil

1 cup sliced yellow onion

1 tablespoon minced garlic

1 tablespoon minced ginger

¼ to ½ jalapeño, chopped

2 Roma tomatoes, each cut into 4 to 6 wedges

1 cup cilantro leaves, coarsely chopped, for garnish

½ cup mint leaves, coarsely chopped, for garnish

Put the tofu in a bowl and coat with half of the spice blend.

Heat a wok or large skillet over high heat. Add 1 tablespoon of the oil and swirl to coat the sides. Stir-fry the tofu until the pieces are lightly browned, about 2 minutes. Transfer to a plate.

Heat the remaining 1 tablespoon oil in the wok. Add the onions and jalapeño and season with the remaining spice blend. Stir-fry briefly, until the onions just start to soften, about 30 seconds. Add the tomatoes and stir-fry briefly. Return the tofu to the wok and cook for 1 minute or just long enough to heat through. The onions should still be firm and crisp in the center (not completely wilted). Serve with cilantro and mint on top.

Tomatoes and onions are classic pairings with steak, but the spice blend used to season this kebat makes the combination even better. Lamb or chicken are also easy substitutions. If using chicken, use 1 pound boneless, skinless chicken breasts (about 2 small breasts), sliced across the grain. The chicken may need to be cooked for a minute or two longer than specified to ensure the meat is cooked through.

Slice the meat thinly across the grain into strips. If the strips are long (more than 4 inches), cut them in half. Transfer the meat to a bowl and use your hands to mix the meat thoroughly with half of the spice blend. Let marinate at room temperature while you prepare the other ingredients.

Heat a wok or large skillet over high heat. Add 1 tablespoon of the oil and swirl to coat the sides. Stir-fry the meat until the pieces are lightly browned but not fully cooked, about 2 minutes. Transfer to a plate.

Heat the remaining 1 tablespoon oil in the wok. Add the onions and jalapeño and season with the remaining spice blend. Stir-fry briefly, until the onions just start to soften, about 30 seconds. Add the tomatoes and stir-fry briefly. Return the meat to the wok and cook for 1 minute or just long enough to cook the meat through. The onions should still be firm and crisp in the center (not completely wilted). Serve with cilantro and mint on top.

RESTAURANT-STYLE STEAK KEBAT

SERVES 3; 4 AS PART OF A LARGER MEAL

1 pound steak, such as tri-tip or flank steak

Kebat Spice Mix (see page 81)

----

2 tablespoons canola oil

----

1 cup sliced yellow onion

¼ to ½ jalapeño, sliced

----

2 Roma tomatoes, each sliced into 4 to 6 wedges

----

1 cup cilantro leaves, coarsely chopped, for garnish

½ cup mint leaves, coarsely chopped, for garnish

The main difference between a home-style shrimp kebat and a home-style meat kebat is that the shrimp version uses ginger and shrimp paste. To go full Burmese, use tamarind water instead of lime to perk up the dish before serving. This dish is just as good with a neutral, relatively firm white fish with a medium flake, such as rockfish or catfish. For a spicier kebat, add one or two minced Thai chiles with the garlic and ginger.

HOME-STYLE SHRIMP KEBAT

SERVES 3; 4 AS PART OF A LARGER MEAL

1 pound large shrimp (16–20 or 20–25 per pound), peeled and deveined, or boneless, skinned fish fillets, such as rockfish, cut into ½-inch pieces

----

1 teaspoon Madras curry powder

----

1 teaspoon fish sauce

½ teaspoon salt

----

1 small-to-medium yellow onion

----

2 tablespoons canola oil

----

1 tablespoon minced garlic

----

1 tablespoon minced ginger

----

1 teaspoon shrimp paste (optional, see page 238)

----

2 Roma tomatoes, each cut into 6 to 8 wedges

----

2 tablespoons Tamarind Water (page 218) or 1 lime, cut into wedges

----

Cilantro sprigs, for garnish

In a bowl, use your hands to mix the shrimp with the curry powder, fish sauce, and salt. Let the shrimp marinate at room temperature while you prepare the other ingredients.

Halve, peel, and core the onion. Slice half of the onion thinly, and finely dice the remaining half. Set the onion slices aside to add at the end.

In a wok or large skillet, heat the oil over medium-high heat. Add the diced onion and cook until softened, 3 to 4 minutes. Stir in the garlic, ginger, and shrimp paste and cook for 2 minutes more.

Add the shrimp and cook, stirring occasionally, over medium heat for 2 minutes. (If using fish, cook for 5 to 6 minutes or until the fish is cooked through and is nearly starting to flake apart.) Gently mix in the sliced onions and tomatoes and cook for 1 to 2 minutes more. The onions should still be firm and crisp in the center (not completely wilted). Finish with the tamarind water or a couple of squeezes of lime. Serve with cilantro on top.

Served with a side of plain jasmine rice, chicken kebat is Burmese home cooking at its simplest. Desmond's mom wonders why it even requires a recipe. This is one of those dishes that you can easily pull together on a weeknight. To spice things up, add a minced Thai chile or a dried chile.

Slice the chicken into strips no wider than a ½ inch. Transfer to a bowl and use your hands to mix the chicken with the curry powder, fish sauce, and salt. Let the chicken marinate at room temperature while you prepare the other ingredients, or refrigerate it overnight.

Halve, peel, and core the onion. Slice half of the onion thinly, and finely dice the remaining half. Set the onion slices aside to add at the end.

In a wok or large skillet, heat the oil over medium-high heat. Add the diced onions and cook until softened, 3 to 4 minutes. Stir in the garlic and cook for 1 minute more.

Add the chicken and cook over medium heat for about 5 minutes. Add the water and continue to cook until the chicken is cooked through and the water has evaporated, about 5 minutes more. Mix in the sliced onion and tomatoes and cook for about 1 minute more. The onions should still be crisp in the center (not completely wilted). Serve with cilantro on top and lime wedges alongside.

HOME-STYLE CHICKEN KEBAT

SERVES 3 TO 4; 6 AS PART OF A LARGER MEAL

1½ pounds boneless, skinless chicken thighs (5 to 6 thighs)

1½ teaspoons Madras curry powder

1 teaspoon fish sauce

½ teaspoon salt

1 small-to-medium yellow onion

2 tablespoons canola oil

2 tablespoons minced garlic

2 tablespoons water

2 Roma tomatoes, each cut into 6 to 8 wedges

Handful of cilantro sprigs, coarsely chopped, for garnish

1 lime or lemon, cut into wedges, for garnish

With cumin and black mustard seeds complementing soy sauce, garlic, and rice vinegar, this dish comes across as Pan-Asian. Yet its roots are Chinese. In north-western China, Uyghur Muslims have used cumin for years, and the spice, while still not that common in the rest of China, makes appearances in lamb stir-fries and grilled meat dishes. Regardless of its historical roots, Chili Lamb has a large and devoted fan base at Burma Superstar.

CHILI LAMB

SERVES 4 AS PART OF A LARGER MEAL

1½ pounds boneless leg of lamb

1 teaspoon cornstarch

¼ teaspoon ground black pepper

½ teaspoon salt

3 tablespoons canola oil

1 teaspoon cumin seeds

1 teaspoon black mustard seeds

1½ teaspoons soy sauce

1½ teaspoons dark soy sauce or regular soy sauce

2 teaspoons unseasoned rice vinegar

1 teaspoon sugar

1 tablespoon minced garlic

2 tablespoons minced jalapeños

3 small dried chiles, seeds retained, broken in half

¼ to ½ teaspoon dried chile flakes

1 cup sliced yellow onion

10 Thai basil leaves, plus extra for garnish (optional)

Trim off the external sinew of the lamb leg. With a knife, separate the muscles by following along where the muscles naturally separate and slice against the grain into thin strips, removing any sinew as you work.

Transfer lamb to a bowl and use your hands to mix the meat with the cornstarch, pepper, salt, and 1 tablespoon of the oil. Let marinate at room temperature while you prepare the remaining ingredients.

In a dry wok or skillet, toast the cumin seeds and mustard seeds until the cumin is fragrant and the mustard seeds start to pop, no more than 30 seconds. Transfer to a mortar and use a pestle (or a coffee grinder used for grinding spices) to pulverize to a coarse powder.

In a small bowl, stir together the soy sauces, 1 teaspoon of the rice vinegar, and the sugar.

Heat the wok over high heat. Add 1 tablespoon of the oil and swirl to coat the sides. Stir-fry the lamb until the pieces have separated and are lightly browned but not fully cooked, about 2 minutes. Transfer to a plate.

Heat the remaining 1 tablespoon of oil in the wok. Add the garlic and jalapeños and cook briefly, about 15 seconds. Add the mustard-cumin blend, chiles, and chile flakes and stir-fry briefly. Pour in the sauce mixture, increase the heat to high, and let the sauce come to a boil.

Add the lamb and onions and cook, stirring often, until the lamb is cooked through but the onions are still slightly crisp, 2 to 3 minutes. Add the basil and the remaining 1 teaspoon vinegar. Taste, adding more soy sauce or vinegar if desired. Garnish with more basil.

NOODLES

Noodles (*khaut swe* in Burmese) are used so often
in salads and soups that it's hard to draw the line between
a noodle dish and a salad.

At the Oakland Burma Superstar, Daw Yee has plated countless orders of Rainbow Salad in the three years she has worked there. A perennial menu favorite, the so-called salad is made with four—four!—different kinds of noodles. That's why it's included in this chapter. Like Rainbow Salad (page 95), Superstar Vegetarian Noodles (page 92) are also served at room temperature—like a salad. This is actually quite common in Myanmar, where even dishes like Nan Gyi Thoke (page 98), rice noodles mixed with coconut chicken curry and topped with hard-boiled eggs, can be served at room temperature. More important than the temperature of the noodle dish is its textural complexity. A good noodle dish has a combination of richness and acidity, soft noodles and crunchy fried bits.

For the uninitiated, the variety of Asian noodles on the market can be intimidating. There are not only so many kinds but also so many names for the same kind of noodle. To help make sense of it all, here's a breakdown of noodle types. If you're having trouble sourcing the exact noodle for a recipe, use what you can find—any kind of rice noodle will work for a rice noodle dish and any Chinese wheat or egg noodle will work for a wheat noodle dish. Chances are the flavors and textures will work just fine.

Rice Noodles

Rice noodles can be either round or flat, and they are sold in various thicknesses. At the store, look for packages of dry round rice noodles, often called "rice stick," or *bun* (the Vietnamese term for a round rice noodle). In this book, these round rice noodles are used in two thicknesses, thin vermicelli style and thick, chewy style.

Fine Rice Noodles: These round rice noodles are thinner than spaghetti but thicker than angel hair. They are great in soups, like Mohinga (pages 115 and 118), and also find their way into the Rainbow Salad. These cook much faster than thicker rice noodles or wheat noodles. For brothy soups, they can be soaked in warm water until soft but still a bit firm. Then all you have to do is drain them, add them to a soup bowl, and top with boiling broth.

Extra-Large or Large Round Rice Noodles: For recipes such as Shan Noodles (page 100) and Nan Gyi Thoke (page 98), look for "Jiangxi rice stick XL" or "L." Found at stores like Ranch 99, Three Ladies Brand makes a good version. If you can't find these round rice noodles, opt for flat rice noodles.

Flat Rice Noodles: Also called *banh pho* noodles because they go into pho, they're also called pad thai noodles because they're sold in pad thai kits, these noodles can stand in for large or extra-large rice stick noodles. They come in various widths, but medium or large work well for the recipes in this book. Annie Chun's pad thai rice noodles are widely available and can be used in place of fine or large round rice noodles.

Glass Noodles

You might see labels that say cellophane noodles, bean thread noodles, or bean thread vermicelli, but they're all more or less the same thing. These noodles are great served cold in salads. In this book, they make an appearance in Rainbow Salad. Burma Superstar uses glass noodles containing mung bean starch, which are more fragile than the kind of glass noodles made with sweet potato starch—those are more common in Korean dishes.

Chinese Wheat Noodles

Burma Superstar uses two kinds of Chinese wheat noodles: flat, ribbon-like noodles and thin round noodles. The flat noodles are the feature ingredient in Garlic Noodles (page 101), while the thin round ones are one of the four noodles used in Rainbow Salad. The restaurant buys flat wheat noodles fresh in large boxes labeled "wonton noodles," and dried lo mein, but don't get stuck on the type if it's hard to find. For the recipes in this book that call for Chinese wheat noodles, anything from "wonton noodle" or "Hong Kong noodle" to plain old "lo mein" will work.

Think of this noodle dish as the vegetarian-friendly version of the Rainbow Salad (page 95), with fewer ingredients to prepare. Since it's served at room temperature, it's a good party dish or a noodle salad to pack for lunch. The fussiest part of making this recipe is frying the onions, garlic, tofu, and wonton wrappers. But if you happen to have Fried Onions, Fried Garlic, and Onion Oil (pages 208 and 211), then all you need to do is fry the tofu and the wontons—if you want to. (Though if you find a bag of fried wonton strips at the grocery store, go ahead and use those instead.) Any neutral oil can be used in place of the onion frying oil mixed into the noodles at the end.

SUPERSTAR VEGETARIAN NOODLES

SERVES 4 TO 6 AS PART OF A MEAL

5 ounces baby potatoes, peeled and quartered

5 ounces firm tofu

¾ cup canola oil

½ cup sliced yellow onion

¼ cup sliced garlic

4 wonton wrappers, sliced into thin strips

12 ounces dried Chinese wheat noodles or 1 pound fresh wonton noodles

½ cup hot water

1 ounce tamarind pulp (see page 238)

Place the potatoes in a small pot, add enough water to cover, and bring to a boil. Decrease the heat to medium-low and cook until tender when pierced with a fork, 15 to 20 minutes. Drain well.

Line a plate with paper towels. Cut the tofu into ½-inch cubes. Put the cubes on the lined plate and put another paper towel over the top, pressing lightly to soak up extra water. Let sit while you prepare the other ingredients.

In a wok or saucepan, heat the oil over medium-high heat. Line a baking sheet with paper towels. Add the yellow onions to the oil, decrease the heat to medium, and cook, stirring often, until the onions have evenly browned and turned crisp, about 8 minutes. If the onions start browning too quickly, turn the heat down to low. With a slotted spoon, lift the onions out and scatter on the paper towels. Set aside 1 tablespoon of the onion frying oil.

Add the sliced garlic to the remaining oil in the wok, decrease the heat to low, and cook, stirring often, until the garlic is an even golden color and nearly completely crisp, about 3 minutes. Lift the garlic out of the oil and place next to the fried onion. Add the tofu to the oil and fry until lightly golden, about 2 minutes. Lift the tofu out and place next to the fried garlic. Scatter the wonton strips in the wok (don't add them in one clump or they'll stick together). Fry until lightly brown and crisp, about 2 minutes. Place the wonton strips next to the tofu.

CONTINUED

2 tablespoons sriracha

1 tablespoon minced garlic

1 tablespoon minced ginger

½ teaspoon salt

¼ teaspoon sugar

1 (5-inch) cucumber (or half an English cucumber), thinly sliced

½ cup thinly sliced red onion, soaked in cold water and drained

2 cups shredded green cabbage

1 cup cilantro sprigs, coarsely chopped

2 tablespoons toasted chickpea flour (see page 215)

Dried chile flakes

1 tablespoon Onion Oil (page 208) or canola oil

1 lime, halved

Bring a pot of water to a boil. Cook the noodles, stirring often with chopsticks, until nearly soft all the way through, about 4 minutes, or until tender but still slightly chewy. Strain the noodles into a colander and rinse under cool running water. Let the noodles drain while making the sauce.

To make the sauce, in a bowl, pour the ½ cup of hot water over the tamarind and let it soak for 5 to 10 minutes, occasionally using your hands or a spoon to mash the pulp and help it dissolve into the water. Strain through a fine-mesh strainer, pressing down on the pulp to extract more tamarind. Stir in the sriracha, minced garlic, ginger, salt, and sugar.

In a large serving bowl, combine the potatoes, noodles, cucumber, red onion, cabbage, cilantro, chickpea flour, and pinches of salt and chile flakes. Drizzle in the saved onion frying oil and squeeze the lime over the top. Fold in the sauce, followed by the fried onions, fried garlic, fried tofu, and wonton strips. Mix well and serve at room temperature.

In Burmese, the original name of this dish translates to "hand-mixed salad," which doesn't do much to explain how gloriously over-the-top and colorful it is. There is saffron-infused rice, four kinds of noodles, cabbage, potatoes, tofu, green papaya, fried onions, fried garlic, tomatoes . . . you get the picture. Years ago, Joycelyn had the genius idea to rename it Rainbow Salad, and the name stuck.

It's true that this dish has a lot of components, but as long as a balance of crunchy to soft ingredients is maintained, it's perfectly okay to omit a few—or get creative and add bits of whatever is in the refrigerator. For instance, if out of left-over rice, skip the saffron rice—there's no need to make rice solely for this salad. If you do happen to buy a green papaya for this recipe, use the remainder in other recipes in the book, like the Chicken Salad (page 133) and the Green Mango Salad (page 130). And if you happen to have a green mango, use it instead of the green papaya. At the restaurants, one order of Rainbow Salad serves up to three people and it's mixed tableside (with utensils). At home, it's easier to make one large salad, mixing everything together—with your hands if you'd like—before putting it on the table. If making it ahead, leave the fried wontons out until ready to serve to prevent them from going soggy.

RAINBOW SALAD

SERVES 6 AS PART OF A LARGER MEAL

¼ cup boiling water

Pinch of saffron threads

Turmeric (optional)

½ cup cooked jasmine rice

5 ounces baby potatoes, peeled and quartered

5 ounces firm tofu

¾ cup canola oil

In a heatproof bowl, pour boiling water over the saffron. Let steep until the water has turned yellow-orange. Add a pinch of turmeric and the rice to the water and mix together.

Place the potatoes in a small pot, add enough water to cover, and bring to a boil. Decrease the heat to medium-low and cook until tender when pierced with a fork, 15 to 20 minutes. Drain well.

Line a plate with paper towels. Cut the tofu into ½-inch cubes. Put on the lined plate and put another paper towel over the top, pressing lightly to soak up extra water. Let sit while you prepare the other ingredients.

In a wok or saucepan, heat the oil over medium-high heat. Line a baking sheet with paper towels. Add the yellow onions to the oil, decrease the heat to medium, and cook, stirring often, until the onions have evenly browned and turned crisp, about 6 minutes. If the onions start browning too quickly, turn the heat down to low. With a slotted spoon, lift the onions out and scatter on the paper towels. Set aside 2 tablespoons of onion frying oil.

CONTINUED

½ cup sliced yellow onion

¼ cup sliced garlic

5 wonton wrappers, sliced into thin strips

1 ounce glass (mung bean) noodles

3 ounces extra-large or large round rice noodles

3 ounces fine round rice noodles

3 ounces Chinese wheat noodles

2 cups shredded green cabbage

1 Roma tomato, diced

1 cup cilantro sprigs, coarsely chopped

½ jalapeño, diced (seeds removed for less heat)

1 cup shredded green papaya (about ¼ of a small papaya)

½ cup thinly sliced red onion or shallot, soaked in cold water and drained

3 tablespoons toasted chickpea flour (see page 215)

2 tablespoons shrimp powder (see page 235)

1 teaspoon dried chile flakes

Salt

¼ cup Tamarind Water (page 218)

Lime wedges (optional)

Add the garlic to the remaining oil in the wok, decrease the heat to low, and cook, stirring often, until the garlic is an even golden color and nearly completely crisp, about 3 minutes. Lift the garlic out of the oil and place next to the fried onion. Add the tofu to the oil and fry until lightly golden, about 2 minutes. Lift the tofu out and place next to the fried garlic. Scatter the wonton strips in the wok (don't add them in one clump or they'll stick together). Fry until lightly brown and crisp, about 2 minutes. Place the wonton strips next to the tofu.

Place the glass noodles in a bowl, add hot tap water, and soak for 10 to 15 minutes or until softened. Drain well.

Meanwhile, bring a pot of water to a boil to cook the rest of the noodles in batches. Cook the extra-large rice noodles, stirring often with chopsticks, until cooked through, about 12 minutes. Lift the noodles out of the water with a spider and drain in a colander. Rinse under cool running water, and shake off the extra water. Transfer to a large mixing bowl. To the pot of boiling water, add the fine rice noodles and cook, stirring often, until cooked through, about 4 minutes. Lift the noodles out of the water with a spider and drain in the colander. Rinse under cool running water, and shake off the extra water. Add to the mixing bowl with the extra-large rice noodles. Add the wheat noodles to the boiling water and cook until cooked through, 4 to 8 minutes, depending on the variety of noodle (use the label for guidance). Drain the noodles in the colander, rinse under cool running water, and shake off the extra water. Add them to the mixing bowl. Drain the glass noodles in the colander and add them to the bowl.

To the noodles, add the saffron rice, potatoes, fried onions, fried garlic, fried tofu, cabbage, tomato, cilantro, jalapeño, papaya, red onions, chickpea flour, shrimp powder, and chile flakes. Season with a few pinches of salt. Drizzle in the saved onion frying oil and tamarind water. Give the salad a good stir with clean hands and taste, adding more salt or squeezing the lime over the top if desired. Serve with fried wonton strips on top for crunch.

Once, while working on this book, we found ourselves at the end of a long day at a new mall development in Yangon. While malls are commonplace in the rest of Asia, this one was a first for Yangon—though it's assuredly a sign of what's to come. We browsed the grocery store on the ground level and then headed upstairs to encounter a lackluster food court with watery Chinese noodles. The only thing worth eating was at the next stall over, a tea shop selling *nan gyi thoke*. Consisting of chewy, round rice noodles lightly coated in a savory chicken curry topped with hard-boiled eggs, it was a perfectly balanced plate of noodles.

Also called Mandalay *mouti thoke*—a tribute to its origin city—and *nan pia thoke* when made with flat rice noodles, nan gyi thoke is a classic Burmese noodle preparation that leverages the richness of Coconut Chicken Curry (page 26). Make it when you have leftover curry, or make a batch of curry specifically for these noodles.

NAN GYI THOKE

SERVES 4 AS PART OF A LARGER MEAL

3½ cups Coconut Chicken Curry (page 26)

Salt or fish sauce

¼ cup toasted chickpea flour (see page 215)

½ teaspoon dried chile flakes

12 ounces extra-large or large round rice noodles

1 lime or lemon, cut into wedges

1 cup sliced red onion or shallot, soaked in water and drained

½ cup minced cilantro

4 hard-boiled eggs (see sidebar, page 21), sliced into wedges

½ cup crispy Fried Onions (page 208)

In a small pot, bring the curry to a gentle simmer. If some of the pieces of chicken are longer than an inch, chop them up and return them to the pot. Taste the curry. It should be rich and savory. Add a teaspoon of salt or a tablespoon of fish sauce if the flavors need more oomph—the noodles will be bland, so all of the seasoning has to come from the sauce. Mix in the chickpea flour and dried chile flakes. If the curry looks broken (with oil rising to the surface), don't worry: just give the pot a good stir.

Bring a pot of water to a boil. Add the noodles and cook, stirring often with chopsticks, 9 to 12 minutes (depending on how thick the noodles are) or until tender but still chewy. If the pot starts to boil over, add a cup of cold water to temper the heat of the water. Drain in a colander and rinse well under cool running water until room temperature. Give the colander a shake to remove excess water.

Transfer the noodles to a large mixing bowl. Add the curry and combine with tongs. Taste, adding a pinch of salt or a splash of fish sauce and a couple of squeezes of lime. Stir in the red onion and cilantro.

Divide the noodles among serving bowls or plates and top each with hard-boiled egg wedges and some fried onions.

If you visit Yangon, chances are your guidebook will direct you to a place serving *Shan khaut swe*—Shan noodles. Originating in Shan State, which borders Thailand and China, Shan noodles are simple and satisfying. Some versions of these noodles are closer to pho, served in a broth with thinly sliced pork. Others are made without broth, topped with a sauce of minced pork or chicken instead—which is the version on the Clement Street menu, a staff favorite. This version, which is also the dry style, comes from Desmond's aunt. The unifying trait of both styles is the bowl of pickled Chinese mustard greens served with the noodles, instantly up the flavor impact. If you don't want to make your own, look for packets in the refrigerated section of Asian grocery stores.

SHAN NOODLES

SERVES 4

1½ pounds boneless, skinless chicken thighs, cut into ¼- to ½-inch pieces

2 tablespoons paprika

½ teaspoon cayenne

½ teaspoon turmeric

1 teaspoon five-spice powder

1½ teaspoons salt

½ teaspoon dried chile flakes

¼ cup canola oil

2 cups minced yellow onion

¼ cup minced garlic

1 tablespoon soy sauce

10 to 12 ounces extra-large or large round rice noodles

¼ cup crushed peanuts

4 green onions (white and green parts), thinly sliced

½ cup Pickled Mustard Greens (page 223)

In a bowl, use your hands to mix the chicken with the paprika, cayenne, turmeric, five-spice powder, salt, and chile flakes. Let the chicken marinate at room temperature while you prepare the other ingredients.

In a heavy pot, heat the oil over medium-high heat. Add the onions and cook, stirring occasionally, until the onions have softened and the edges start to brown, 4 minutes. Stir in the garlic, lower the heat to medium, and cook 3 minutes more.

Add the chicken and cook, stirring often, until the chicken is cooked through and the sauce looks rich and deeply red (thanks to the paprika), about 7 minutes. Lower the heat if the bottom starts to darken too much. Turn off the heat and stir in the soy sauce. Taste, adding more soy sauce or salt if needed (the sauce should taste assertive because the noodles are unseasoned).

Bring a pot of water to a boil. Add the noodles and cook, stirring often with chopsticks to prevent sticking, 9 to 12 minutes (depending on how thick the noodles are) or until tender but still chewy. If the pot starts to boil over, add a cup of cold water to temper the heat of the water. Drain in a colander and rinse briefly under cool running water. Give the colander a shake to remove excess water.

Transfer the noodles to a warmed serving bowl. Pour the chicken and all of the sauce on top and sprinkle with peanuts and green onions. Serve pickled mustard greens alongside.

Some form of this comfort dish is made in nearly every corner of Asia, and it has long been a popular item both in Myanmar and at Burma Superstar. While the noodles, which get their flavor from fried garlic and garlic-infused oil, are respectable on their own, some like to beef up the dish with shredded duck, barbecue pork, sautéed shrimp, or stir-fried mushrooms and broccoli. Anything goes. The trickiest part of making garlic noodles is ensuring the garlic doesn't burn. In this recipe, the garlic is pulled off the heat and left to cool in the oil. If you want to safeguard the process a bit more, set up a heat-proof bowl with a mesh strainer. When the garlic reaches a deep golden color, pour the garlic through the strainer to stop the cooking.

GARLIC NOODLES

SERVES 4

¼ cup canola oil

4 tablespoons minced garlic

¾ cup sliced red onion or shallot, soaked in water and drained

2 tablespoons soy sauce

½ cup sriracha

1 tablespoon minced ginger

¼ teaspoon sugar

¼ teaspoon salt

2 tablespoons water

12 ounces fresh wide wonton noodles or dried Chinese wheat noodles

1 (5-inch) cucumber (or half an English cucumber), thinly sliced

3 green onions (white and green parts), thinly sliced

In a small pot, heat the oil over medium heat. Add 3 tablespoons of the garlic, set the heat to low, and fry, swirling the pot frequently, until the garlic is nearly golden in color, no more than 3 minutes. (If the garlic starts to darken too quickly, pull the pot off the heat, swirl the oil, and let the garlic continue to fry off the heat for 30 seconds before returning it to the heat.) Because the garlic can burn quickly, watch the pot the whole time while the garlic fries.

Immediately pour the oil into a heatproof bowl and let it cool. The garlic will continue to cook and turn golden as it sits. If the garlic is already golden brown before you take it off the heat and it looks like it might burn if left in the hot oil, all is not lost. Pour the oil through a fine-mesh strainer into a heatproof bowl to remove the garlic from the oil and stop it from cooking further. Once the oil has cooled a bit, return the garlic to the oil.

Add the onions and soy sauce to garlic.

In a small serving bowl, stir together the sriracha, the remaining 1 tablespoon of garlic, the ginger, sugar, salt, and water.

Bring a pot of water to a boil. Add the noodles and cook, stirring often with chopsticks, until nearly soft all the way through, about 4 minutes or until tender but still slightly chewy. Drain in a colander and rinse briefly under cool running water. Give the colander a shake to remove excess water.

Return the noodles to the pot. Pour in the garlic–soy sauce mixture and add the cucumbers. Give the noodles a good stir with a pair of tongs, then divide among bowls. Top with the green onions. Serve with sriracha sauce.

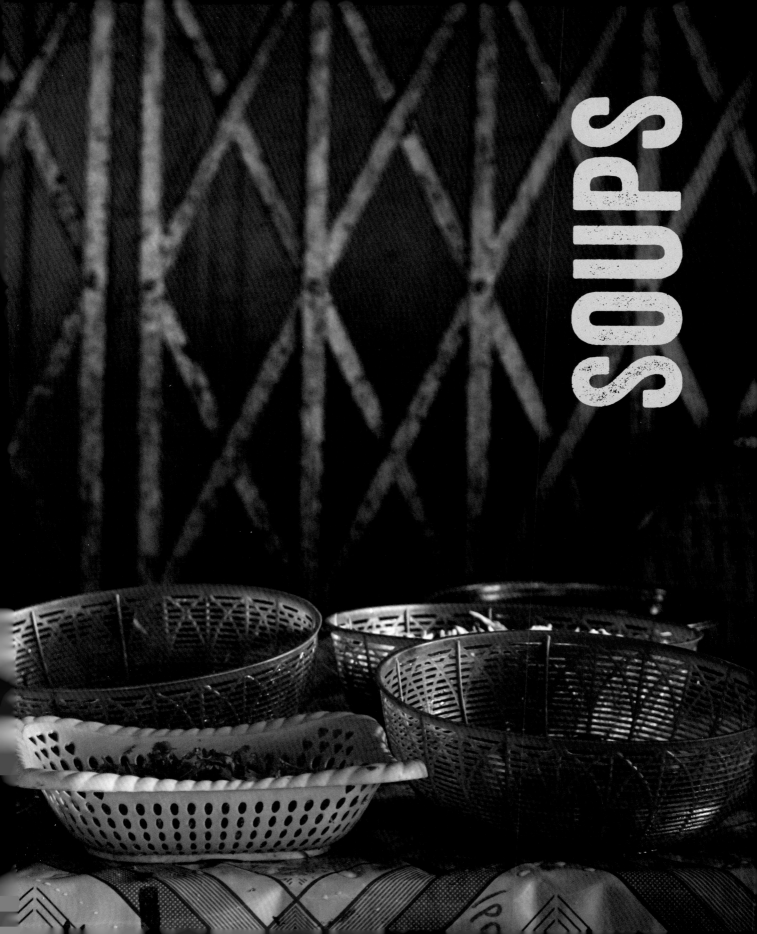

SOUPS

In Myanmar, soups generally fall into two categories. Brothy soup—often made sour with tamarind pulp—is sipped throughout a meal. Some say it stimulates the appetite and helps you eat more rice. The other, heartier kind of soup is substantial enough to be a meal on its own.

The most famous dish in this chapter is *mohinga*, which is by all accounts the country's national dish. On the Burma Superstar menu, Mohinga is one of those sleepers, overlooked in favor of Tea Leaf Salad or Samusa Soup. Yet it's long been a favorite of both Desmond and Joycelyn. And in Myanmar, it's served everywhere from tea shops to fancy hotel buffets to crowded street stalls where people start lining up in the morning for their fix. Consisting of whole catfish cooked in a peppery broth and served with noodles, it's a favorite breakfast food that tastes just as good at other times of the day. In Myanmar, mohinga is so pervasive that every region has its own version. The central part of the country uses freshwater fish, while the coasts use seafood and inland areas use chicken. It's such an important dish that we included two recipes in this book: Classic Mohinga and Rakhine Mohinga, a spicier version from the coastal Rakhine State.

While classic European-style soups are thickened with a roux made of flour and butter, hearty Burmese soups tend to rely on chickpea flour or toasted, ground rice to thicken the broth. It's a clever trick that feels completely modern, especially for anyone who cooks gluten-free. But it's also great for flavor, as neither thickener masks the main ingredients of the soup. And some soups, like Chin Corn Soup, are closer to porridge than soup (yellow hominy, beans, and greens make a filling—and absurdly healthy—meal).

The key to success with the recipes in this chapter is working ahead and simplifying when necessary. For this reason, toppings are provided as nice-to-have, not need-to-have, options. The soups can stand alone without them. You can also make the toppings a day or two ahead. For the mohingas, Coconut Chicken Noodle Soup, and Samusa Soup, the bases can be made the day or two before the soup is served. No matter what you do, always add your noodles right before serving so they don't overcook in the broth.

For whatever reason, Burmese-English menus often write samosas with a "u" instead of an "o"—hence Samusa Soup. Yet a bowl of this soup—whether served in Yangon or San Francisco—includes more than those namesake savory fried filled pastries (however you want to spell them). There are also fried bits of potato and fritters made with yellow split peas (what Burma Superstar employees call falafel). Brimming with South Indian flavor, it is by far the most popular soup on the menu.

The most important component is the broth. Toasted chickpea flour thickens it while curry powder and garam masala add fragrance. If making samosas and falafel for the sole purpose of this soup is a tall order, skip them; make the broth and add a cup of cooked diced potato for a simple, healthy alternative. The broth, samosas, and falafel freeze well, so you can make the various recipes at different times, freeze them, and then serve them all together down the road. If you have the Mustard-Cumin Spice Blend (page 215), you can use 2 teaspoons of it in place of the cumin seeds and mustard seeds called for here.

SAMUSA SOUP

SERVES 4 TO 6

Soup

1 teaspoon cumin seeds

1 teaspoon black mustard seeds

⅓ cup canola oil

4 small dried chiles

3 bay leaves

2 cups finely diced yellow onion

¼ cup minced garlic

1½ teaspoons paprika

½ teaspoon turmeric

2 teaspoons salt

1 teaspoon Tamarind Salt (page 217; optional)

¼ cup toasted chickpea flour (see page 215)

6½ cups water

½ cup Tamarind Water (page 218)

½ jalapeño or 2 Thai chiles, minced

½ teaspoon Garam Masala (page 216)

¼ cup loosely packed, torn mint leaves

Serving

6 Samosas (page 188), at room temperature

6 Yellow Split Pea Falafel (page 191), at a warm room temperature

2 cups shredded green cabbage

1 cup cilantro sprigs

1 lime, cut into wedges

In a dry wok or skillet over medium heat, toast the cumin and mustard seeds until the cumin is fragrant and the mustard seeds start to pop, no more than 30 seconds. Transfer to a mortar with a pestle or a coffee grinder and pulverize to a coarse powder.

In a heavy pot, heat the oil over medium-high heat. Add the mustard-cumin blend, dried chiles, and bay leaves and cook briefly to draw out the aromas, 20 seconds. Stir in the onions and garlic, lower the heat to medium, and cook, stirring frequently, until the onions are softened, 5 minutes. Stir in the paprika, turmeric, salt, and tamarind salt and cook for 3 minutes more or until the water has been cooked down and a thin film of oil rises to the surface.

In a small bowl, whisk together the chickpea flour and ½ cup of the water until the flour no longer has lumps. Stir the flour mixture into the pot. Pour in the remaining 6 cups of water and the tamarind water and bring to a boil. Lower to a simmer and cook for 15 minutes. Stir in the jalapeño, garam masala, and mint. Taste the broth—you may want to add more salt or a squeeze of lime. (At this point, you can cool the broth and refrigerate for up to 1 week or freeze for up to 1 month.)

To serve, break up the samosas and falafel into pieces and divide among 4 large bowls or 6 small bowls. Ladle the hot broth over the top. Top with shredded cabbage and cilantro, and serve lime wedges on the side.

This brothy soup gets its pucker from sour leaf (pictured here and page 110, also see page 50), a favorite green among the Burmese. You don't have to wait to find sour leaf to make this soup though. A mix of sorrel leaves and spinach leaves can be used in its place with the help of tamarind water. But keep your eyes peeled for fresh sour leaf. Or ask a Burmese friend where to buy it frozen.

This soup makes for a light lunch with rice served on the side or it can be served in small bowls as part of a larger meal. To make it richer, add thinly sliced lotus root. For the fish, any kind of white-flesh variety—catfish, cod, or rockfish—will do. Or skip the fish and use peeled and deveined shrimp.

SOUR LEAF SOUP

SERVES 4 TO 6 AS PART OF A LARGER MEAL

12 ounces boneless, skinned white fish fillet, such as rockfish

1¼ teaspoons salt

¼ cup canola oil

2 cups finely diced yellow onion

2 tablespoons minced garlic

2 teaspoons shrimp paste (see page 238)

1 teaspoon paprika

½ teaspoon cayenne

½ teaspoon turmeric

2 to 3 Thai chiles, each cut crosswise into 3 pieces

4 cups firmly packed fresh, stemmed sour leaf; or 1 cup frozen and thawed sour leaf (about 1 bunch); or 4 cups spinach and 2 cups stemmed and coarsely chopped sorrel leaves

Trim away any bones from the fish fillets. (Rockfish fillets often have a set of ribs running halfway down the center. Simply slice down both sides of the bones to cut them out.) Cut the fish into ½- to 1-inch pieces. Transfer to a bowl and mix with a ½ teaspoon of the salt. Let sit at room temperature while you prepare the other ingredients.

In a 4-quart pot, heat the oil over medium-high heat. Stir in the onions and cook, stirring often, until the onions have browned around the edges and softened, 4 minutes.

Stir in the garlic and continue to cook, stirring occasionally, until the garlic is very aromatic, about 2 minutes. Stir in the shrimp paste and cook for 1 minute.

Stir in the paprika, cayenne, turmeric, chiles, and the remaining ¾ teaspoon salt and cook briefly, about 30 seconds. Add the fish and stir to coat in the aromatics. (It's okay if the fish begins to break into smaller pieces.)

Add the sour leaf, packing it down so it all fits in the pot, and cook until wilted if fresh and warmed through if frozen, about 4 minutes. If it has been previously frozen, use a spoon to break up the chunks. If it's fresh, stir it to encourage the leaves to wilt.

CONTINUED

Add the fish sauce, water, and tamarind water and bring to a boil. Lower to a simmer and stir in the sliced onions. Cook for 3 minutes more. By now, the fish should be fully cooked and the sliced onions softened but still slightly crunchy. Taste, adding more fish sauce, tamarind water, or salt as needed. Ladle into bowls and garnish with cilantro.

1 tablespoon fish sauce

4 cups water

¼ cup Tamarind Water (page 218)

½ cup thinly sliced yellow onion or shallot

10 cilantro sprigs, for garnish

If you like Coconut Chicken Curry (page 26), try this noodle soup, which is essentially the same curry in soup form. *Ohn no khaut swe* is probably one of the most popular soups in Myanmar among tourists, especially those who are fans of Thailand's *khao soi*, a soup that is similar enough for some to say it evolved from this Burmese classic. For yet another variation on the coconut chicken noodle theme, try the *Nan Gyi Thoke* (page 98).

COCONUT CHICKEN NOODLE SOUP

SERVES 4 TO 6

Soup

1½ pounds boneless, skinless chicken thighs

----

1 tablespoon paprika

----

2 teaspoons turmeric

½ teaspoon cayenne

----

2 teaspoons salt

¼ cup canola oil

----

2 cups finely diced yellow onion

¼ cup minced garlic

----

2 tablespoons minced ginger

----

2 (13½-ounce) cans unsweetened coconut milk

----

3 tablespoons fish sauce

4½ cups water

¼ cup toasted chickpea flour (see page 215)

----

10 to 12 ounces flat rice noodles

Trim the chicken thighs and cut into ½-inch pieces. Transfer to a bowl and use your hands to mix with the paprika, turmeric, cayenne, and salt. Let marinate at room temperature while you prepare the other ingredients.

In a heavy 6-quart pot, heat the oil over medium-high heat. Stir in the onions, decrease the heat to medium-low, and cook, stirring often to prevent scorching, for 8 minutes or until the onions are very soft and have started to brown at the edges. Add the garlic and ginger and cook for 2 minutes more.

Add the chicken and stir to release the spices into the onions. Pour in the coconut milk and bring to a near boil. Let the coconut milk simmer briskly for about 8 minutes. Decrease the heat to medium-low and add the fish sauce. Stir in 4 cups of the water and bring the pot back to a near boil.

In a small bowl, whisk together the chickpea flour and the remaining ½ cup water until no lumps remain. Stir into the broth.

Lower the soup to a gentle simmer and cook, stirring occasionally, until the chicken is tender, 50 to 55 minutes. If time permits, let the soup sit for at least 20 minutes before serving. This allows the chicken to become tender and to soak in the flavor of the soup as it cools.

To cook the noodles, bring a pot of water to a boil. Add the noodles and cook, stirring often with tongs or chopsticks to prevent sticking, 5 to 6 minutes or until softened. Turn off the heat and let the noodles sit in the water for 3 minutes. Drain in a colander, rinse under cool running water, and give the colander a shake to remove excess water. If not serving right away, mix some canola oil into the noodles with your hands to keep them from sticking together. (You can also cook the noodles in advance and soak them in warm water before serving to loosen them up.)

To serve, divide the noodles among the bowls. Bring the soup to a simmer and taste, adding more salt or fish sauce if desired. Ladle the soup over the noodles and top with the hard-boiled eggs, chile flakes, and cilantro. Serve lime wedges alongside.

Serving

2 hard-boiled eggs (see sidebar, page 21), sliced into wedges

Dried red chile flakes

1 cup cilantro sprigs, coarsely chopped

1 lime or lemon, cut into wedges

CLASSIC MOHINGA

SERVES ABOUT 6

Unless you've been to Myanmar or have a Burmese friend, you've probably never heard of *mohinga*, which is too bad: it's essentially the national dish, made in nearly every corner of the country. When sister restaurant Burma Love was newly opened, Desmond noticed the mohinga served there wasn't quite hitting the mark. To troubleshoot, he asked Ma Htay, one of the restaurant's cooks who had been working on the salad station, to show the other cooks where they were going wrong. She nailed it.

Ma Htay grew up in Thanlyin, a city across the river from Yangon. She worked at a factory there until she and her husband and daughter secured a diversity visa to come to the United States. Ma Htay started cooking when she was ten years old, beginning with rice and working her way up to fried eggs until she finally learned how to make mohinga. The trick to this classic dish is achieving the right balance of ingredients, from the toasted rice powder to the freshness of the fish. And classic mohinga should contain lemongrass to counteract the fishy aroma. In Myanmar, Ma Htay says, lines form at the mohinga stalls that get the ratio of ingredients correct. Each mohinga is built to order: the noodles (cooked separately) go into the bowl first, followed by a ladleful of soup and a handful of toppings that you can choose from. At home, mohinga is made in a big pot on special occasions. The richer you are (so the logic goes), the more fish you add to the pot.

The mild lemongrass-infused broth is thickened with toasted rice that is ground to a powder. A clean coffee grinder works well for grinding the rice. This recipe uses whole catfish, the bones of which add flavor and body to the broth. Fitting a whole catfish in a pot can be tough, though, so ask the fishmonger to cut it into thirds, retaining all the bones and the head, or be prepared to bend the fish to get it to fit in the pot. The fish flesh is later removed from the bones and mashed into a paste with aromatics, losing its shape. (Customers ordering mohinga for the first time often ask where the fish is.)

Classic mohinga is not typically a spicy bowl of noodles. For a spicier version, try the Rakhine Mohinga (page 118). When selecting bay leaves, avoid fresh California bay laurel leaves and opt for milder bay leaves at Indian and Southeast Asian markets or leave them out. Use any or all of the garnishes suggested here.

CONTINUED

½ cup uncooked jasmine rice

Broth

3 quarts water

3 stalks lemongrass (see page 228), cut into 3-inch pieces

2-ounce piece ginger (unpeeled), thickly sliced crosswise into slabs

5 bay leaves

1½ teaspoons ground black pepper

½ teaspoon ground white pepper

2 teaspoons salt

1 scaled and gutted catfish (about 3 pounds)

Soup

⅓ cup vegetable oil

1 stalk lemongrass, minced (see page 228)

¼ cup minced garlic

3 tablespoons minced ginger

1 tablespoon paprika

1 teaspoon turmeric

2 red onions, diced into ½-inch pieces (about 3½ cups)

¼ cup fish sauce

Salt

10 ounces fine round rice noodles

Heat the oven to 350°F. Spread the rice across a rimmed baking pan and bake, giving the pan an occasional stir, until the rice is an even golden color and aromatic, 20 minutes. Cool to room temperature and then pulverize in a clean coffee grinder.

To make the broth, select a large wide pot that will fit the catfish comfortably with room to spare. (An 8-quart pot works well.) Add the water, lemongrass, ginger, bay leaves, black and white pepper, and salt and bring to a boil. Lower the heat and simmer for 15 minutes.

Carefully lower the fish into the pot. The fish may not be completely covered in water, but that's okay. Bring the pot to a brisk simmer, lower the heat, and cook gently for 15 minutes. Using tongs, carefully turn the fish over or at least rotate it slightly to cook the side that was sticking out of the water. Simmer for another 5 minutes or until the fish flesh pulls away cleanly from the bone. Using tongs and a spider or slotted spoon, lift the fish out of the broth and transfer to a bowl. Turn off the heat and let the broth sit on the stove.

When the fish is cool enough to handle, pull off the skin and discard. Separate the cooked fish from the bones, trying to keep the skeleton (or skeleton portions if the fish is cut in pieces) intact. Set aside the cooked fish. Return the skeleton (including head and tail) to the pot.

Bring the pot to a boil. Lower the heat and simmer for 15 minutes. The broth should have a mild ginger-lemongrass flavor and be slightly cloudy. Strain the broth through a fine-mesh strainer. You will have about 10 cups. Give the pot a quick rinse (when it's cool enough to handle), and return the broth to the pot.

In a small bowl, whisk together the powdered rice and a ladleful of the broth until no lumps remain. Stir into the broth. Bring the broth to a simmer and cook, stirring often, until it starts to barely thicken, about 5 minutes. Turn the heat to low and cook the broth at a gentle simmer while preparing the soup.

To make the soup, in a wok or large skillet, heat the oil over high heat. Add the lemongrass, garlic, and ginger and stir-fry for 1 minute. Add the cooked fish, paprika, and turmeric, mashing the fish gently with a spoon to turn it into a coarse paste, and cook for about 1 minute. If you see any errant bones, pick them out.

Pour the contents of the wok into the broth and bring to a brisk simmer. Add the red onions and fish sauce. Simmer for 5 minutes more or until the flavors start to come together. Taste the broth: it should be on the salty side because the noodles will not have any salt. If it's not that salty, add some salt or fish sauce. (At this point, the soup can be cooled and served the next day.)

To cook the noodles, bring a pot of water to a boil. Add the noodles and cook, stirring often with tongs or chopsticks to prevent sticking, for 5 to 6 minutes or until softened. Turn off the heat and let the noodles sit in the water for 3 minutes. Drain in a colander, rinse under cool running water, and give the colander a shake to remove excess water. If not serving right away, mix some canola oil into the noodles with your hands to keep them from sticking together. (You can also cook the noodles in advance and soak them in warm water before serving.)

To serve, divide the noodles among the bowls. Ladle the soup over the noodles and serve the hard-boiled eggs, crackers, cilantro, and lime wedges alongside.

Serving

6 hard-boiled eggs (see sidebar, page 21), sliced

12 Yellow Split Pea Crackers (page 184), broken into pieces

½ cup chopped cilantro

2 limes, cut into wedges

Thinly sliced red onions

Rakhine State hugs the Bay of Bengal, and mountains on its eastern border cut it off from central Myanmar. Their coastal location means the residents of Rakhine State cook with ocean-caught fish instead of catfish, like they do in inland Myanmar. And while geography doesn't quite explain it, Rakhine food uses a sweat-inducing amount of chiles and pepper. Even the most innocuous-looking fish salads can deliver a punch. These two elements are on display in the Rakhine version of mohinga. This soup isn't overpoweringly spicy, but it goes heavy on black pepper. It's also brothier than classic mohinga, which helps alleviate some of the heat.

When making Rakhine Mohinga at home, choose any whole, non-oily fish you like. Whole tai snapper is a good option. It's okay if the fish is smaller or larger than 3 pounds. Ask your fishmonger to gut, scale, and cut the fish in half or thirds. This makes it easier to fit the fish in the pot. (If the fish is kept whole, you'll just need to bend it to fit into the pot.) Ginger and *galangal* (a similar-looking rhizome with a clean flavor; see page 227) are both classic ingredients in Rakhine Mohinga, though you can leave the galangal out and double down on the ginger. What really sells this dish to heat-seekers at the table is sprinkling raw minced Thai chiles and garlic over the top before eating.

RAKHINE MOHINGA

SERVES ABOUT 6

Broth

3 quarts water

----

2 yellow or red onions, diced into ½-inch pieces (about 3½ cups)

One to two 3-ounce pieces ginger (unpeeled), thickly sliced crosswise into slabs

----

2 tablespoons shrimp paste

----

2 tablespoons minced galangal (optional)

To make the broth, select a large wide pot that will fit the fish comfortably with room to spare. (An 8-quart pot works well.) Add the water, onions, ginger, shrimp paste, galangal, salt, pepper, turmeric, chopped chiles, and bring to a boil. Lower the heat and simmer for 15 minutes. The shrimp paste should break down in the broth.

Carefully lower the fish into the pot. The fish may not be completely covered in water, but that's okay. Bring the pot to a brisk simmer, lower the heat, and cook gently for 8 to 10 minutes. If necessary, using tongs, carefully turn the fish over or at least rotate it to cook the side that was sticking out of the water and cook for a few minutes more or until the fish flesh pulls away cleanly from the bone, a total of 12 to 15 minutes for tai snapper but longer for catfish. Using tongs and a spider or slotted spoon, lift the fish out of the broth and transfer to a bowl. Turn off the heat and let the broth sit on the stove.

When the fish is cool enough to handle, pull off the skin and discard. Separate the cooked fish from the bones, trying to keep

CONTINUED

1½ tablespoons salt

---

1 tablespoon ground black pepper

½ teaspoon turmeric

---

2 chopped serrano chiles
or 2 to 5 Thai chiles, halved

---

1 scaled and gutted fish (about
3 pounds), such as tai snapper

Soup

⅓ cup canola oil

---

2 cups minced yellow onion

⅓ cup minced garlic

---

1 tablespoon minced ginger

---

1 tablespoon minced galangal
(optional)

---

1 teaspoon turmeric

---

1 teaspoon salt

½ cup Tamarind Water (page 218)

---

10 ounces fine rice noodles

Serving

¼ cup minced garlic

¼ cup minced Thai, jalapeño,
or serrano chiles

1¾ cups Fried Onions (page 208)

A large bowl of cilantro sprigs

---

the skeleton (or skeleton pieces if the fish is cut in pieces) intact. Set aside the cooked fish. Return the skeleton (including head and tail) to the pot.

Bring the pot to a boil. Lower the heat and simmer for 15 minutes. The broth should have a ginger flavor and be on the salty side. Strain the broth through a fine-mesh strainer. You will have about 10 cups. Give the pot a quick rinse (when it's cool enough to handle) and return the broth to the pot. Turn the heat to low and cook the broth at a gentle simmer while preparing the soup.

To make the soup, in a wok or large skillet, heat the oil over high heat. Add the onions and cook for 4 minutes or until softened. Add the garlic, ginger, and galangal and stir-fry for 1 minute. Add the cooked fish, turmeric, and salt, mashing the fish gently with a spatula or spoon to turn it into a coarse paste, and cook for 1 to 2 minutes. If you see any errant bones, pick them out.

Pour the contents of the wok into the broth and bring to a brisk simmer. Simmer for 5 minutes more or until the flavors start to come together. Add the tamarind water. Taste the broth: it should be assertive because the noodles are unseasoned. If it tastes underseasoned, add more salt. (At this point, the soup can be cooled and served the next day.)

To cook the noodles, bring a pot of water to a boil. Stir in the noodles and cook, stirring often with tongs or chopsticks to prevent sticking, for 5 to 6 minutes or until softened. Turn off the heat and let them sit in the water for 3 minutes. Drain in a colander, rinse under cool water, and give the colander a shake to remove the excess water. If not serving right away, mix some canola oil into them with your hands to keep them from sticking together. (You can also cook the noodles in advance and soak them in warm water before serving.)

To serve, divide the noodles among the bowls. In a small bowl, stir together the garlic and chiles. Ladle the soup over the noodles and serve the garlic-chile mixture, fried onions, and cilantro alongside.

This hearty porridge comes from Nang Khan Cin—"Afoo"—who heads the kitchen at the Alameda location of Burma Superstar. Ethnically Chin, he left Myanmar to seek work in Malaysia before eventually coming to Oakland with the help of the International Rescue Committee (IRC). Afoo was the first cook Desmond hired from the IRC program. Everyone who is Chin has their own version of this simple soup, which is brought to life by mixing roasted tomatoes, ginger, garlic, and chiles together like salsa.

For this soup, look for dried golden hominy, which looks like broken popcorn kernels, in Mexican or Asian grocery stores. The brand Goya makes one. In Chinese grocery stores, it's called "dried broken corn." If you find only canned hominy, look for "golden corn hominy," and give it a rinse before using. (If you have super-artisanal hominy, read the label to see if it requires further treatment before it can be cooked.) The recipe calls for small red beans, which can be anything from pinto to kidney to borlotti (cranberry) beans.

CHIN CORN SOUP

MAKES 6 SERVINGS

Soup

8 ounces golden hominy or dried broken corn

8 ounces dried small red beans

1 tablespoon salt

About 8 cups leafy greens, such as chard, collard greens, or red or green amaranth (for chard and collards, cut the thickest part of the stems into small pieces; for amaranth, remove the thick stems)

In separate bowls, cover the hominy and the beans with 2 inches of water and soak overnight at room temperature. Drain. Add both soaked ingredients to a 6-quart or larger pot and cover with 1 inch of water.

Bring to a boil. Lower to a gentle simmer and cook, stirring occasionally, until the hominy and beans are cooked through, about 1½ hours. Add more water to the pot halfway through to ensure the hominy and beans stay covered. To check for doneness, cut a kernel of hominy in half and split a bean in half. If either is still chalky in the center, keep simmering.

When the hominy and beans are done, stir in the salt and greens and add more water if the soup is as thick as oatmeal (although the soup should not be watery). Simmer for 10 minutes more or until the grains, beans, and greens are fully integrated. Taste, adding more salt if needed. The soup will taste bland, but it will come to life when eaten with the salsa.

Meanwhile, make the pounded sauce. Preheat a broiler. Line a rimmed baking sheet or pan with aluminum foil and place the tomatoes on the foil. Broil until the tomato skin starts to blister,

CONTINUED

3 to 4 minutes. Rotate the tomatoes and broil for another 3 to 4 minutes or until most of the skins have blistered. (Alternatively, char the tomatoes on a grill.) Coarsely chop the tomatoes.

In a mortar with a pestle, mash the ginger, garlic, and chile together into a coarse paste. Add the salt and cilantro and mash some more. Add the tomatoes and continue to mash until a chunky salsa forms. Taste, adding more salt if needed (the sauce should taste assertive to bring flavor to the hominy and beans).

To serve, ladle the soup into the bowls and serve the sauce alongside. Before eating the soup, heap a generous spoonful or two of the sauce on top, and continue to add sauce as you eat.

Pounded Sauce

4 Roma tomatoes

2-inch piece ginger, peeled and coarsely chopped

3 garlic cloves, crushed

1 jalapeño chile, coarsely chopped (seeds removed for less heat)

1 teaspoon salt

½ cup coarsely chopped cilantro

CHIN STATE

Many of the Burmese refugees who have come to Oakland are from the Chin State, a mountainous region bordering India and the home of the Chin people, one of Myanmar's minority groups. The Chin State is a remote and difficult place to live, especially when the monsoon rains wash away roads and leave people stranded without food. In the summer of 2015, when we were in Myanmar researching this book, the flooding in the Chin and Rakhine states was so severe that bags of rice and other aid relief were piled up in the domestic terminal of the Yangon airport, their distribution routes washed out.

While Chin food may be elusive in Myanmar, the influx of Chin refugees in the United States is opening up this world to Americans. Chin food is simple and healthy, brimming with leafy greens, tomatoes, chiles, eggplant, and potatoes. Some find it similar to Nepalese food. Rice is rare, but beans and hominy grow easily there and are used in simple, hearty soups.

SALADS

Burmese salads—*thoke*—are completely original.
To fully understand them, however, you need to abandon the
idea that all salads are a mix of lettuce and vegetables with
dressing. This is not the land of balsamic vinaigrette.

There are a couple of reasons why salads are so pervasive in Myanmar. For starters, nearly anything can be turned into a salad. Leftover fried chicken? Make a salad. Samosas from the day before? Slice them up, toss them with cabbage and tamarind water, and you have another salad. Even jerky can be turned into a salad. While on the hours-long drive to Namhsan, the prime tea-growing region in the Shan State, we stretched our legs at a roadside stop serving dried mutton jerky as a salad—shredded and tossed with lime, shallots, and a bit of crushed garlic.

The second reason salads are so important is that they require little from a limited kitchen. If a curry is cooking on the only charcoal burner available, a salad can be tossed together without any need for heat. Peanuts can be mashed in a mortar and pestle and then mixed into a salad of tender fresh tamarind leaves (a must-try salad on any trip to Myanmar). That doesn't mean these are simple plates: one of the most popular salads served street-side in Yangon is a variation of Rainbow Salad (page 95), which is an everything-but-the-kitchen-sink noodle salad.

The most famous of these dishes is *laphet thoke*, tea leaf salad. *Laphet*, the star ingredient, is made by fermenting just-picked tea leaves for months (see page 143). It creates a dark green "dressing" that lightly coats the rest of the ingredients. While laphet is the highlight, this salad also showcases another key component of all good Burmese salads: texture. It's full of fried lentils, seeds, garlic, dried shrimp, chickpea flour, and tomato.

These salads are not difficult to put together, but they require planning. The first step is tracking down and preparing the components.

The second part is learning how to compose the salad. Instead of being dressed with a vinaigrette, for instance, these salads are put together by mixing all of the ingredients with some of the oil used to fry onions or garlic. Tamarind water and citrus juice are used to balance out the savory flavors. Toasted chickpea flour often lightly coats the ingredients, thickening the salads just like grated Parmesan enriches a Caesar salad. Having these basics ready to go before you start makes all the difference.

For this book, start with the Ginger Salad and Green Mango Salad before working your way to bigger projects, like Tea Leaf Salad. And don't be afraid to mix and match ingredients—like swapping out cucumber for fried garlic chips or skipping peanuts—to tailor the salads to suit your tastes. The most important part is giving the salad a good mix before serving. While servers at the restaurants mix the salads with forks at the table, don't be shy about using your hands (in true Burmese style) when mixing these salads at home. With the exception of the tea leaf salad (which gets a bit messy), it's the best way to ensure that all the flavors and textures are evenly blended together.

With pickled ginger as the key component, this refreshing salad makes a good counterpoint to any rich curry or stir-fry, especially Pumpkin Pork Stew (page 33) or Chili Lamb (page 86). Japanese pickled ginger is not hard to find at well-stocked grocery stores (opt for white pickled ginger instead of pink, if possible). You can also make your own (see sidebar). It is especially good when made with young ginger—if you are lucky enough to come across it. Like all good Burmese salads, this recipe does not skimp on all the crunchy bits. Keep them on hand to make more of this salad—you may want to eat it all week. If you happen to have any Ginger Juice (page 161) left over from making drinks, add a splash to the bowl as you mix the salad.

GINGER SALAD

**SERVES 4 AS PART
OF A LARGER MEAL**

4 cups thinly sliced romaine lettuce (about 1 romaine head)

1½ cups shredded cabbage

3 heaping tablespoons thinly sliced pickled ginger, chopped

2 tablespoons Fried Garlic Chips (page 211)

3 tablespoons Fried Yellow Split Peas (page 213)

3 tablespoons coarsely chopped cilantro

2 tablespoons sunflower seeds

2 tablespoons coarsely chopped toasted peanuts

2 tablespoons minced jalapeños

1 tablespoon toasted sesame seeds

1½ tablespoons toasted chickpea flour (see page 215)

1½ tablespoons Onion Oil (page 208) or canola oil

2 tablespoons juice from the ginger pickling liquid

2 teaspoons fish sauce (optional)

¼ teaspoon salt

1 lime or lemon, cut into wedges

In a salad bowl, combine the lettuce, cabbage, pickled ginger, fried garlic, split peas, cilantro, sunflower seeds, peanuts, jalapeños, and sesame seeds. Sprinkle chickpea flour over the top and drizzle with oil and pickling liquid. Add the fish sauce and salt (use more salt if you are not using fish sauce). Squeeze 1 or 2 lime wedges over the top. Using your hands, mix well and taste, adding more salt or lime juice if needed.

MAKING PICKLED GINGER

The best pickled ginger is made with young ginger, but even mature ginger can be pickled. Older ginger will likely be spicier, so you may want to use less of it.

Peel a 3-inch piece of ginger (about 1½ ounces). Slice it very thinly into planks with a sharp knife or a mandoline and transfer to a heatproof container. In a small saucepan over medium heat, combine 2 tablespoons sugar, 5 tablespoons distilled white vinegar, and 2 tablespoons water, stirring until the sugar dissolves. Pour the mixture over the ginger and let it cool to room temperature. Refrigerate until needed.

Instead of relying only on lime or lemon juice, Burmese salads often use other tart ingredients as a way to bring acidity to salads. In this salad, green mangoes are up for the task. Although available at Asian grocery stores year-round, these underripe mangoes are at their peak in the spring. For the best tart flavor, look for smaller mangoes with smooth, green skin free of blemishes. You won't need to use a whole green mango to make this salad, so keep extra fried onions, peanuts, and chickpea flour on hand to make this recipe again with the rest of the mango. Or use the mango in the Rainbow Salad (page 95) in place of the green papaya. Alternatively, you can buy green pickled mango in brine that's already been sliced into strips (it's often dyed a yellow color). Avoid Indian-style green mango pickle, which is packed in oil and is a completely different condiment.

GREEN MANGO SALAD

SERVES 4 AS PART OF A LARGER MEAL

½ green mango, peeled

4 cups thinly sliced romaine lettuce (about 1 romaine head)

1 cup shredded cabbage

½ cup thinly sliced cucumber

⅓ cup Fried Onions (page 208)

¼ cup thinly sliced red onion or shallot, soaked in water and drained

3 tablespoons coarsely chopped cilantro

2 tablespoons coarsely chopped toasted peanuts

2 tablespoons minced jalapeño

1½ tablespoons toasted chickpea flour (see page 215)

1 teaspoon fish sauce (optional)

¼ teaspoon salt

2 tablespoons Onion Oil (page 208) or canola oil

1 lime or lemon, cut into wedges

Slice the mango into thin planks, then slice the planks crosswise into thin matchsticks. You should have about ½ cup sliced green mango.

In a salad bowl, combine the mango, lettuce, cabbage, cucumbers, fried onions, red onion, cilantro, peanuts, jalapeño, and chickpea flour. Add the fish sauce and salt (use more salt if you are not using fish sauce). Drizzle with the oil and squeeze 1 or 2 lime wedges over the top. Using your hands, mix well and taste, adding more salt or lime juice if needed.

This is more evidence that in Burmese cooking, everything can be turned into a salad. The best chicken to use here is leftover cooked chicken—simply pull the leftovers into pieces. Fried chicken or rotisserie chicken is great for this salad. If you do need to cook chicken for this salad, poaching it is the easiest way to go. For 1 large chicken breast or 2 to 3 chicken thighs, put the chicken in a small pot and cover with water. Bring to a boil, season the water with a few generous pinches of salt, and then lower the pot to a simmer and cook for 15 minutes. Turn off the heat, cover the pot, and let the chicken steep for 30 minutes. The chicken will finish cooking as it rests.

CHICKEN SALAD

SERVES 2; 4 AS PART OF A LARGER MEAL

½ yellow onion, thinly sliced

1 lime, halved

3 tablespoons canola oil

About 2 cups cooked chicken (about 2 rotisserie chicken breasts or 1 large chicken breast, poached), at room temperature

1 cup shredded cabbage and/or romaine lettuce

½ cup thinly sliced cucumber

2 tablespoons seeded and minced jalapeño

2 tablespoons coarsely chopped cilantro

1½ tablespoons toasted chickpea flour (see page 215)

1 teaspoon fish sauce

¼ teaspoon salt

1 teaspoon Fried Garlic Chips (page 211), crushed (optional)

Put a quarter of the sliced onion in a small bowl. Squeeze half a lime on top and mix to coat.

In a wok or skillet, heat the oil over medium-high heat. Add the remaining quarter of a sliced onion, lower the heat to medium, and cook, stirring often, until the onion has evenly browned and turned crisp, about 10 minutes.

Pour the onion and the frying oil into a large mixing bowl. Once the oil has cooled to room temperature, top with the chicken, cabbage, cucumbers, jalapeño, cilantro, and chickpea flour. Add the fish sauce, salt, and reserved raw onion with the lime juice. Using your hands, mix well. Taste, adding more fish sauce, more lime juice, or a pinch of salt if needed. Transfer to a salad bowl and sprinkle fried garlic on top.

Mount Popa is a temple that sits atop an extinct volcano jutting out of the plains like an oversized thumb. About a half-day's trip from the archaeological sites of Bagan, Popa is home to thirty-seven *nats*, Myanmar's indigenous spirits, as well as a bunch of bored monkeys. If you go during the slow season (March through October), don't bring food while climbing the 777 steps (barefoot) to get to the top—and if you do, anticipate getting cornered by some of the beefier chimps demanding the goods. The photographer for this book, John Lee, had to sacrifice his water bottle to get out of a jam. For all we know, these monkeys are merely acting on the will of the nats.

Down the road from the temple are a few restaurants serving travelers who have come to pay Popa a visit. One of those places served up this salad. Green tomato salads are common in Myanmar, with the sour underripe tomatoes playing well against sweet crushed peanuts and peanut oil. After the sweltering hike to the summit, the salad was both cooling and satisfying. If you grow tomatoes, keep this salad in mind for the beginning and end of the season, when it's easiest to access green tomatoes. You can go all green, or mix and match green and red; cherry tomatoes are fine here too.

GREEN TOMATO SALAD

SERVES 4 AS PART OF A LARGER MEAL

2 tablespoons peanut oil

1 Thai chile, cut into 3 or 4 pieces

¼ teaspoon dried chile flakes

5 green tomatoes (about 1 pound)

½ cup thinly sliced shallot

2 garlic cloves, smashed flat with the blunt side of a knife blade

3 tablespoons crushed roasted peanuts

1 lime, halved

Salt

1 cup cilantro sprigs

In a very small saucepan, heat the oil briefly with the chile and the chile flakes. Pour into a small bowl and let sit while you prepare the other ingredients.

Slice the tomatoes into thin wedges and transfer to a bowl. Add the shallots, garlic, peanuts, reserved chile oil, and a generous couple of pinches of salt. Squeeze half of the lime over the top. Using your hands, mix well and taste, squeezing more lime over the salad or adding more salt if needed. Put the salad and any juices onto a rimmed serving plate and garnish generously with cilantro sprigs.

Samusa Salad may be the most underappreciated salad on the Burma Superstar menu—but if it's ever taken off the menu, its fans will be crushed. It's actually surprising that its fan base isn't bigger: it's hard not to like the combination of crunchy samosas and shredded cabbage drizzled with a tamarind ginger dressing. Besides, the idea of using samosas in salad isn't so different from using bread to make croutons. If you're not inclined to make samosas, buying some at the store and popping them in the oven to make this salad works just fine. If you happen to have any Samusa Soup (page 106) on hand, spoon some of the broth over the salad for a richer flavor.

SAMUSA SALAD

SERVES 2; 4 AS PART OF A LARGER MEAL

4 Samosas (page 188), sliced

2 cups shredded cabbage and/or romaine lettuce

½ cup sliced cucumbers

⅓ cup Fried Onions (page 208)

¼ cup thinly sliced red onion or shallots, soaked in water and drained

2 tablespoons seeded and minced jalapeños

3 tablespoons coarsely chopped cilantro

2 tablespoons coarsely chopped mint

1 tablespoon toasted chickpea flour (see page 215)

½ teaspoon salt

2 tablespoons Onion Oil (page 208) or canola oil

2 tablespoons Tamarind Ginger Dressing (page 219) or Tamarind Water (page 218)

1 lime or lemon, cut into wedges

In a salad bowl, combine the samosas, cabbage, cucumbers, fried onions, red onion, jalapeño, cilantro, mint, chickpea flour, and salt. Drizzle with the oil and tamarind dressing and squeeze 1 or 2 lime wedges over the top. Using your hands, mix well. Taste, adding more salt or lime juice if needed.

This is another one of those uniquely Burmese salads that makes you rethink what a salad really is. In this case, it's silky chickpea tofu mixed with crunchy fried garlic and onions and a tamarind ginger dressing. The combination may seem unusual, but it's easily one of the more refreshing things to eat on a hot afternoon in the tropics. First make the Shan Tofu; one batch will allow you to make two of these salads. Or use half of the tofu to make a salad and deep-fry the other half to eat as a snack.

SHAN TOFU SALAD

SERVES 2; 4 AS PART OF A LARGER MEAL

½ yellow onion, thinly sliced

½ lime

Half a recipe (about 8 ounces) Shan Tofu (page 185), thinly sliced

2 tablespoons Fried Garlic Chips (page 211), crushed slightly

1 Thai chile, thinly sliced (optional)

½ teaspoon dried chile flakes

1 tablespoon toasted chickpea flour (see page 215)

2 tablespoons Tamarind Ginger Dressing (page 219) or Tamarind Water (page 218)

½ cup coarsely chopped cilantro, plus sprigs for garnishing

3 tablespoons canola oil

½ teaspoon salt

Put a quarter of the sliced onion in a small bowl. Squeeze the lime on top and mix to coat.

In a salad bowl, combine the tofu, fried garlic, fresh and dried chiles, chickpea flour, tamarind dressing, and chopped cilantro.

In a wok or skillet, heat the oil over medium-high heat. Add the remaining onion, lower the heat to medium, and cook, stirring often, until the onion has evenly browned and turned crisp, about 10 minutes.

Pour the fried onions and the frying oil into the bowl with the tofu. Once the oil has cooled to room temperature, add the reserved raw onion with the lime juice. Add the salt and cilantro sprigs. Using your hands or a spoon, mix gently to evenly coat all the pieces. Taste, adding more salt if needed.

When heading to Namhsan from Lashio or Mandalay, there is only one true roadside stop before beginning the three-hour-plus climb up the mountain. It's a no-frills place with cell phone advertisements pasted on the walls, dusty dried goods on display, and a small open-air kitchen in the back. But it serves a decent menu, which you can wash down with tea or Myanmar beer. One day, while working on this book, we shared an order of this salad, intrigued by the inclusion of shredded dried mutton. On our way back down the mountain, we stopped at the place again, this time ordering two plates and heading to the kitchen to watch them put it together. We named this salad after that jewel-in-the-rough joint, Namhsan Restaurant.

The dried mutton used in Myanmar is hung to dry as it cures and then is fried or smoked. Since sheep jerky is hard to come by in the United States, this recipe has been modified to use beef jerky. Look for a variety that's on the firm, savory side. Teriyaki and Asian barbecue flavors tend to be too sweet. To shred the jerky, simply pull it into pieces along the grain so you get longer strips. A little jerky goes a long way, so while this salad only makes a small portion, it's best to share it as part of a larger meal. It can also be made ahead.

NAMHSAN SALAD

**SERVES 4 AS PART
OF A LARGER MEAL**

1 cup thinly sliced shallot

2 limes, halved

2 tablespoons peanut oil or canola oil

2 small dried chiles, broken
into pieces

2 cups loosely packed shredded
beef jerky (about 6 ounces)

½ to 1 Thai chile, minced

1 garlic clove, coarsely chopped

Salt

Put the shallot in a small bowl. Squeeze 1 lime on top and mix to coat.

In a very small saucepan, heat the oil with the dried chile until the chile just begins to crisp and darken, about 1 minute. Pour into a mixing bowl and let cool to room temperature.

Add the jerky, Thai chile, garlic, and a pinch of salt. Using your hands, mix well and taste, squeezing in more lime or adding salt if needed.

EAT YOUR TEA: THE STORY OF MYANMAR'S MOST MYSTERIOUS FOOD

Tea shops around Yangon and Myanmar pour gallons of green tea and black tea every day. Yet half of the tea consumed in Myanmar is eaten, not drunk. Made by fermenting just-picked Assam leaves, *laphet*—or what the Burmese call "pickled tea"—is slightly bitter, deeply savory, and strangely addictive.

It's remarkable that laphet makes it to the States at all. For years, the fermented tea leaves were nothing more than a mysterious dark green product brought back in suitcases after trips to Southeast Asia. Trade embargos made it impossible to import it directly from Myanmar. Yet the method of fermenting tea leaves for eating has been practiced for centuries among mountain tribes living in the border regions of Myanmar, China, and Thailand. It's a very old food that somehow, through word of mouth and restaurants like Burma Superstar, has become popular as the main ingredient of one of the most curious Burmese dishes served in America—tea leaf salad.

Part of the draw is novelty. For so long, to get the tea, you needed to know someone who knew someone. Many Americans have tried to make laphet in the States with dried green tea leaves only to find the results didn't come close to the original. Fortunately, it's becoming easier to find the real deal.

NAMHSAN

A few years ago, Desmond started asking around Yangon for information on how laphet (pronounced *la-PET*) is made. He wanted to learn more about the whole supply chain, but no one would give him a direct answer. After coming to several dead ends, he finally got a lead from Bryan Leung, a well-connected Yangon native. Leung had met a guy who had started a tea growing association in Shan State. That guy, Nelson Rweel, turned out to be the key to unlocking the laphet mystery.

Nelson is part of Myanmar's emerging entre-preneurial class. Trained as a teacher, he now runs a chain of English-language schools scattered across the country. Yet his family roots are in tea. He grew up in Namhsan, a rural township in Shan State where tea growing and processing is the lifeblood of the ethnic Palaung community. There are other areas of production in Shan State and Kachin State too. But in the world of edible tea, the laphet from Namhsan is considered the best in the country. And the best laphet within Namhsan comes from Zayan, a village in the northern part of the township.

Getting to Namhsan is not easy. By air from Yangon, you fly to Lashio, the closest airport. From Lashio you drive four or five hours on mostly dirt roads, climbing more than 1,000 meters (3,280 feet) in elevation, passing through fog, and encountering the occasional Burmese military truck. (Rebel armies are also active in these parts.) By road from Mandalay, it's a seven-hour bus ride to Namhsan. During the monsoon season, getting stuck in the

red clay mud is part of the experience. The same main road that snakes up the mountains also connects all of the villages. Storefronts and homes are set up right against the road, without room for much of a sidewalk. Some villages are only accessible by mule. The challenge of getting anything to and from Namhsan is more than merely an inconvenience: in the spring of 2016, a devastating fire tore through the area, burning down homes and businesses and displacing more than 1,000 people. Fire trucks had to come from as far away as Lashio on that same road, and the rebuilding effort is ongoing.

When you finally do arrive, however, the view is breathtaking: mountaintops poke through the fog and everything slows down. Ruby Hill, a Buddhist temple filled with golden pagodas, glimmers in the distance like a tiny version of Yangon's famous Shwedagon. At sunrise, novice monks walk down dirt paths behind the main road, ringing a bell and collecting donations of rice for the monastery. At sundown, the doors and windows close up with heavy shutters, muffling sounds of Burmese soap operas and singing competitions playing on TVs. It's damp at night but pleasantly cool. When we arrived at dusk in August 2015, the air spelled relief, like when the fog rolls into San Francisco after a series of hot days.

GROWING TEA

There's a Burmese adage about the country's most prized foods that goes something like this: if it's meat, it's pork; if it's fruit, it's mango; and if it's leaf, it's tea. It's hard to overstate the importance of tea

in Myanmar, and it's especially hard to overstate the importance of laphet to the Palaung people of Namhsan.

"The only thing we know is the tea leaf business," U Aung Gyi, a laphet producer, told us when we visited his warehouse. Like many others in Namhsan, he wore a pink Palaung head wrap.

Assam is the main tea variety grown here, but compared with the carefully cultivated Assam plantations in India, Burmese Assam is much wilder, with bushes of various sizes clinging to hillsides. The yields are also significantly lower than in India. Grown with no pesticides, Assam tea from Namhsan is naturally organic. Nelson Rweel calls it "jungle tea."

For laphet, tea bushes need eight to ten years to reach maturity. After that, the plants can grow for years, turning tree-size. (We were told—but couldn't confirm due to an impassable road—that there was an 800-year-old tea tree nearby.) While the surrounding areas have heavy red clay soil, the soil in Namhsan is mainly a mix of sand and clay. And in Zayan, it's mostly all sand. This sandy soil and the pitch of the hills (45 degrees is ideal) ensure good drainage. The resulting equation will sound familiar to anyone who knows a little about making fine wine: making the plant struggle a little to hold onto water means lower yields and more concentrated flavor.

The leaves from Zayan-grown tea also have a higher concentration of antioxidants, which helps preserve color and flavor. So while other laphet turns brown or black as it ages, Zayan laphet remains shades of gold. To test the quality, you rub the leaves between your hands and then inhale. Zayan laphet has a sweet, tropical smell, almost like an overripe mango.

The flavor concentration for any tea varies depending on what time of year the leaves are picked. In Namhsan, the first harvest happens in the hot, dry months of March and April, when the buds are small and have the most concentrated flavor. The second harvest, from May to June, is also good quality but not as desirable as the first. The third—from August and September—is the least flavorful thanks to the rains that pass through that time of year and dilute the crop. In some years, there's a fourth harvest in the fall after the rains have stopped. Its quality is nearly as good as the first harvest but lower in yield.

There is no sugar-coating the physical nature of picking tea. One farmer we watched had a bag slung over his shoulder and a basket strapped to his back with a sickle tucked into a strap at his waist. Years of picking the buds of tea plants have made his forearms sinewy with muscle. Women and men pick tea together. At the end of the day, they make their way by foot, mule, truck, or scooter to the processing facility.

MAKING LAPHET

At the processing facility, fermentation starts the day the tea leaves have been picked before they can oxidize and turn black. The tea is steamed, pressed to release excess water, and then rolled. The next day, it's sorted by hand, with the smaller, higher-quality leaves separated from the larger leaves that stay in the local market. Then the tea is packed tightly in plastic-lined burlap sacks, packed down into the bags, and placed in cement containers in the ground. Weights—mostly heavy rocks—are put on top to help compress the leaves. The bags stay there to ferment for at least four months or up to two years, depending on demand from wet tea brokers in Mandalay. While the tea ferments, ink-black oil seeps out of the leaves, staining the bags.

For years it was common for brokers in Mandalay to hold off paying tea farmers and laphet makers for their goods until they sold the products. Brokers took a huge margin. Then there were problems at the tea farms. There wasn't enough money coming in.

"Up until 1995, our tea price was very good," Nelson said. "Farmers didn't have to work too hard.

Now younger farmers want to move to cities for more money." Some tea farms have been abandoned. And since tea farming is seasonal, there's a chunk of time—from October to April—where no one is harvesting. If cash isn't coming in, it's easy to see why there's a temptation to grow opium poppies during the off-season. (Part of the Shan State is in the Golden Triangle.)

Nelson started the tea grower co-op in 2013, to strengthen growers' bargaining rights and organize members to recognize the value of having a naturally organic product. With the help of Desmond and a laphet company called Shan Shwe Taung, he has also brought in trainers from Nepal and Holland to help farmers learn better ways organically to care for tea plants all year long. As countries like the United States lifted trade sanctions, international trade has provided better export opportunities. But for Nelson and his co-op, this has also meant protecting the place names of Namhsan and Zayan from being used to sell inferior tea.

"This is the first time we market our tea to the world," Nelson told a meeting of co-op members in August 2015. Women and men attended, and most of the men wore the pink Palaung head wraps. Some were eating sunflower seeds and many were drinking tea. "We need to do it right and honestly."

HOW TO EAT YOUR TEA

There is no question that laphet is beloved in Myanmar, where it is sold in snack packets or served after a meal in special lacquerware. The place to sample the best laphet is Mandalay, the country's main tea-trading city. Plus, the Burmese say eating tea cools you down, and on steamy summer days in Mandalay, you'll do whatever you can to cool off.

Downtown Mandalay is a chaotic place, a mix of scooters buzzing around a dusty hodgepodge of low-rise buildings, but the tea shops are excellent. Wet—edible tea—shops sell laphet in a number of ways, from whole-leaf laphet to laphet that's been crushed and seasoned with various flavors. (Ginger and garlic is a popular combination.) They also sell all the condiments you might want to eat along with it, from toasted sesame seeds to fried garlic, fried peanuts, and dried shrimp.

One of the best-known brands is Shan Shwe Taung. The company was started by U San Aung, who years ago started to bypass brokers to buy directly from Namhsan farmers. The efforts allowed him to become proficient in understanding the differences in quality. Now his son, Myo Win Aung, has taken over the company, which does brisk business in laphet snack packs, the foil packets that hang like bags of chips at shops across the country.

Eating laphet can be as simple as ripping open a packet and eating it with a few crunchy bits. Its caffeine kick makes it popular with students. When money is tight, some will turn a packet into a meal by eating it over plain rice. Serving laphet in a salad is a little more special, but the best laphet is still reserved for serving in lacquerware after a meal. To aid digestion, guests help themselves to a little whole-leaf laphet and season it however they choose from the crunchy bits, toasted sesame seeds, and tiny whole garlic cloves offered at the table. When you first bite into a tea leaf, you mostly taste bitterness. But if you leave it in your mouth long enough—especially if it's the good stuff—the bitterness mellows, revealing a purely Burmese—and addictive—flavor.

FAKING IT

There's no easy way to fake the savory flavor of laphet. But by brewing a pot of green tea and saving the leaves, you can get close—kind of.

The hardest part is coaxing out of dried green tea an overripe, bamboo shoot–like aroma that resembles laphet. But leaving used tea leaves out at room temperature for a day or two can help. Once blended with ginger and garlic, they make a nice tea paste for a salad. It's lighter and more like pesto than laphet, but it still supplies a little caffeine buzz.

To try it, put 2 tablespoons good-quality loose-leaf green tea, such as Chinese Dragon Well or Japanese sencha, in a cup. Add hot water (about 190°F, just below a boil) and steep for 3 minutes to make a cup of tea. (Go ahead and drink the tea; it's not needed for the paste.) Press out excess water from the leaves, and transfer to a glass or plastic container. Partially cover and leave at room temperature for 2 days. The tea should take on an aroma resembling overripe fruit.

Mince 1 clove of garlic and a teaspoon's worth of ginger and place in a food processor. Add the tea leaves and ¼ teaspoon salt and pulse briefly to break up the leaves. Drizzle in 3 tablespoons canola oil and season with 1 teaspoon distilled white vinegar. At this point, the blend is ready to be used in the Tea Leaf Salad recipe, but refrigerate it overnight for a deeper flavor.

TEA LEAF DRESSING

In Myanmar, you can buy tea leaves in jars or foil packets that can be stored in the refrigerator for at least a year. After years of hearing customers lament the lack of retail sources for fermented tea leaves, Burma Superstar started selling jars of laphet dressing in 2014 at the restaurants and in stores. The main point is to keep your eyes out because laphet is becoming more available in stores and online.

To turn tea leaves into a dressing for salad, Burmese cooks crush them with oil and seasonings in a mortar and pestle. A brief whirl in a food processor also gets the job done. The key is knowing what kind of laphet you're working with before you start. Some packs already have salt and even flavorings while others are sold unseasoned. Before you start, taste the tea leaf. If it tastes bitter, with no noticeable salt, it has not been seasoned and you'll need to add salt. You may also be able to tell if it's seasoned by its weight. A ¼ cup portion of unseasoned whole-leaf laphet will weigh just under 1 ounce. In comparison, seasoned, more pastelike laphet will weigh upward of 1½ ounces for a ¼ cup. If the unseasoned tea leaf is very bitter, soak it for a few minutes in cold water. You can also buy laphet dressing, which already has oil and seasoning blended in; if you do, skip this recipe and instead use the amount called for in the recipes on page 154 and 155. Extra paste keeps for about 6 months in the refrigerator. It may darken or turn brown, but it will still be fine to eat.

For those who are still far from a reliable source, we offer a close facsimile (see opposite page).

Tea Leaf Dressing

½ packed cup (about 2 ounces) whole fermented tea leaves (laphet) or ⅓ packed cup seasoned tea leaf paste (without oil)

⅓ cup canola oil

1 garlic clove, coarsely chopped

¼ teaspoon dried chile flakes

1 teaspoon lime or lemon juice

Salt

If using whole, unseasoned laphet leaves, soak them for 5 minutes in cold water to extract some of the bitterness. Drain, squeezing the leaves to remove excess water. Taste the leaves. If they still taste extremely bitter, soak and drain again. Skip this step if using a seasoned paste.

Put the leaves or paste in a food processor with the garlic and chile flakes and pulse a few times. Add the lemon juice and half of the oil, briefly pulse, and then, with the processor running, drizzle in the rest of the oil. If the leaves are not preseasoned, add 1 teaspoon salt. If the leaves are already seasoned, add only a pinch or two of salt. You will have about ½ cup of tea leaf dressing.

It's hard to pinpoint exactly why tea leaf salad—*laphet thoke*—is so addictive, but it has something to do with its singular combination of textures and savory, salty, mildly sour flavors—and, of course, the caffeine kick you get after eating it. This version of laphet thoke is served in a large bowl with heaps of peanuts, toasted sesame seeds, crispy garlic, fried yellow split peas, tomato, jalapeño, and shredded lettuce. The textures and flavors all enhance the deep umami quality of the laphet.

TEA LEAF SALAD

(LAPHET THOKE)

SERVES 4 AS PART OF A LARGER MEAL

6 cups thinly sliced romaine lettuce (about 1½ heads romaine)

½ cup **Tea Leaf Dressing** (page 153)

¼ cup **Fried Garlic Chips** (page 211)

¼ cup **Fried Yellow Split Peas** (page 215)

¼ cup coarsely chopped toasted peanuts

¼ cup toasted sunflower seeds

1 tablespoons toasted sesame seeds

1 Roma tomato, seeded and diced

1 small jalapeño, seeded and diced (about ¼ cup)

1 tablespoon shrimp powder (see page 235)

2 teaspoons fish sauce or a few generous pinches of salt

1 lemon or lime, cut into wedges

To make the salad, place a bed of lettuce in the center of a large plate or platter. Spoon the tea leaf dressing into the center of the lettuce. Around the lettuce, arrange separate piles of fried garlic, split peas, peanuts, sunflower seeds, sesame seeds, tomato, and jalapeño. Sprinkle with shrimp powder and drizzle with fish sauce. Before serving, squeeze 2 lemon wedges over the plate. Using 2 forks, mix the ingredients together until the tea leaves lightly coat the lettuce. Taste, adding more lemon or fish sauce at the table, if desired.

This is the recipe to make when you happen to have leftover jasmine rice and have found a source for laphet. With shrimp paste, it's a more pungent take on tea leaf salad with deeper umami flavor. For a spicier version, add half a minced Thai chile. Served at room temperature, it exemplifies the Burmese tradition of making a delicious plate of food out of a few odds and ends.

TEA LEAF RICE SALAD

SERVES 4 AS PART OF A LARGER MEAL

1 cup shredded cabbage

½ teaspoon shrimp paste

1 teaspoon water

2 teaspoons fish sauce

¼ cup Tea Leaf Dressing (page 153)

3 cups cooked jasmine rice (about 1 cup uncooked)

¼ cup Fried Onions (page 208)

3 tablespoons Fried Garlic Chips (page 211)

3 tablespoons toasted sunflower seeds

3 tablespoons toasted crushed peanuts

¼ cup coarsely chopped cilantro

1 lime, halved

Salt

To make the salad, place the cabbage at the base of a serving bowl. In a mixing bowl, mix the shrimp paste with the water and the fish sauce to break up the paste.

Microwave the rice briefly if it's cold from the refrigerator. If it's just cooked, scoop the rice out of the rice cooker or pot. Add the rice to the shrimp paste and fish sauce. Mix in the tea leaf dressing. Gently fold in the fried onions, fried garlic, sunflower seeds, peanuts, and cilantro. Squeeze the lime over the top and mix well. Taste, seasoning with salt or more fish sauce if desired. Spoon into the bowl with the cabbage and serve.

DRINKS

Drinking culture in Myanmar is more of a daytime caffeinated experience than a nighttime boozy one. (Government cronies have traditionally controlled most of the country's alcohol business, and everyone generally goes to bed early.)

And tea shops, open-air establishments filled with tables and low wooden stools, are at the center of it all. Teahouses operate from six in the morning to about eight at night and are mostly staffed with kids who come from the countryside and work in exchange for room and board. Each table has a complimentary flask of light green tea, but most who visit order a cup of Myanmar tea, which is brewed strong and lightened with evaporated and condensed milk. The tea itself is made from the kind of Assam black tea you find in English tea bags. It's boiled briefly so that when it's poured through a strainer into a cup, it looks like tea espresso.

A tea shop's reputation is built on the quality of tea served and the tea maker's ability to customize each order to a tea drinker's preference. Very sweet means lots of condensed milk, while unsweetened means no condensed milk. The tea maker combines the condensed milk (or not) with evaporated milk to mellow the tannic bite of the tea. This combination—astringent, earthy tea mixed with shelf-stable milk—results in an addictive toffee-like drink.

The best tea shops are in Mandalay, which serves more black tea than anywhere else in the country. No matter the time of day, kettles are always simmering with nets filled with black Assam tea.

But like everything else in the country, tea shops are changing. The average bill at a teahouse is about $1.50, but rents in Mandalay and Yangon continue to rise. To keep up, shop owners have expanded the menus. At Shwe Pyi Moe Café, a popular Mandalay tea shop with a couple of locations, you can order plates of samosas, bowls of *mohinga* soup, and just-griddled *platha* bread. Still, tea remains the main draw. The tea maker spoons condensed milk into small ceramic cups and then pours in evaporated milk. He then tops off the cups with tea. To froth each cup, he pours the contents back and forth between metal tins. While the drink is similar to Indian chai and Hong Kong milk tea, the flavor of the tea itself is distinctly Burmese.

The Burmese also make a lot of juices with fresh fruit, turning watermelon and papaya into smoothie-like drinks served over ice. It's also common to drink yogurt over ice, often sweetened with honey. Even beer gets the ice-in-the-glass treatment. Cocktails are a bit harder to come by, though that's likely going to change. Who knows? Maybe in a few years, cocktails like the ones served at Burma Superstar will become popular over there, too.

While simple syrup made with white sugar works just fine in cocktails, adding mildly caramel-tasting palm sugar gives the drink a little more complexity. Use the lighter-colored Thai palm sugar, which comes in 3-inch rounds.

PALM SUGAR SYRUP

MAKES ABOUT ²/₃ CUP

4 ounces Thai palm sugar
(about 3 rounds)

½ cup water

In a small saucepan, combine the sugar and water and bring to a boil. Cover, decrease the heat to low and gently simmer, stirring occasionally and breaking up the palm sugar with a spoon, until the sugar has nearly dissolved, 3 to 5 minutes. Uncover and simmer until the sugar has dissolved completely, 1 or 2 minutes more. Let cool to room temperature. Simple syrup keeps refrigerated for at least 3 months, if not longer.

A few recipes in this book call for ginger juice, but if you really like the stuff, you may want to make a bigger batch to keep on hand so Ginger Honey Tea (page 165) or even a round of ginger-infused gin and tonics can be put together in a snap. At the Oakland restaurant, the bar staff use an industrial juicer to pulverize countless knobs of ginger into this fresh juice. At home, you don't need a heavy-duty juicer. Just chop up the ginger, blitz it in a food processor, and then squeeze the juice out of the pulp. Don't get too ahead of yourself, though. Ginger juice is best used within a few days.

GINGER JUICE

MAKES ABOUT ⅔ CUP

10 ounces ginger (unpeeled is fine)

Cut the ginger into chunks and put in a food processor. Let the processor run for a minute or so to make sure all the ginger pieces are thoroughly pulverized. At this point, the ginger juice will still be in the pulp.

To extract the juice from the pulp, line a bowl with a fine-mesh strainer. (If you don't have a fine-mesh strainer, line the strainer or a colander with cheesecloth.) Scoop the pulp into the strainer. Using your hands, press the pulp to release the juice. Some sediment and pulp will go through the strainer, and that's okay—you can re-strain later. Once all the pulp has been squeezed, discard it and re-strain the juice. Store in the refrigerator until using.

When serving this tea, keep in mind that this is strong and best consumed in small doses (Burmese teacups are much smaller than American mugs). For the best flavor, use loose Assam tea with the consistency of ground coffee (not whole leaf). Look for it in Indian grocery stores that sell ingredients for chai, but opt for tea without spices mixed in. Alternatively, select English tea bags, like PG Tips or Tetley. Evaporated milk in the United States has a sweeter milky flavor than the evaporated milk in Myanmar. The best option is Black & White, the brand with the black-and-white-cow on the label that many use for making Hong Kong milk tea. Condensed milk sold at Asian grocery stores also has a less milky flavor than condensed milk sold to the American or Mexican market, and it is closer in flavor to what is used in Myanmar. Look for brands like Longevity, which is used in Vietnamese iced coffee.

If you want to make larger batches, use 1 black English tea bag or 1 tablespoon loose black tea for each additional 6 ounces of water. Any extra tea can be chilled and served over ice.

MYANMAR TEA

SERVES 4

18 ounces water

3 tablespoons loose black Assam tea or 3 English tea bags

4 cups evaporated milk

1 tablespoon condensed milk

Fill 4 small teacups or mugs with hot water to heat them up.

Have a small fine-mesh strainer and heatproof liquid measuring cup ready. In a small pot, bring the water to a simmer. Add the tea and simmer gently for 3 minutes. Strain the tea into the heatproof liquid measuring cup, pressing on the tea solids or tea bags to extract all of the tannins and flavor.

Pour both types of milk into the same pot used to boil the tea. Heat gently, whisking occasionally, until hot. (Avoid scorching the bottom of the pot.)

Pour the tea into the pot with the milk and whisk, frothing the milk. Dump the hot water out of the teacups and ladle in the tea.

During cold and flu season—even if you're feeling fine—it's hard to beat this spicy herbal "tea" made with fresh ginger juice and honey. Make a larger batch of Ginger Juice with the help of a food processor (see page 161) or follow the instructions below for grating a smaller amount. Like Myanmar tea, plan on serving ginger tea in small cups. If you want to get fancy, use a vegetable peeler to shave off a piece of orange rind and add it to the teapot.

Fill 2 teacups or small mugs with hot water to warm them up.

Set a microplane grater across the top of a bowl and grate the ginger, allowing the bowl to catch the pulp. Gather the pulp up and press through a fine-mesh strainer into a cup. (The small strainers used for steeping tea in Japanese teapots work well.) You will have about 2 tablespoons of juice.

In a small teapot or heatproof pitcher, combine the ginger juice and honey. Pour in the boiling water and give it a stir. Taste, adding more honey to sweeten or more water to cut the ginger flavor.

GINGER HONEY TEA

SERVES 2

1½ ounces peeled ginger

3 tablespoons honey

2 cups boiling water

Anyone familiar with Mexican agua de Jamaica will recognize this drink. Made from hibiscus flowers (which come from the same plant family as Myanmar's beloved sour leaf), this sipper is supernaturally magenta, and its pleasant sour flavor goes so well with a meal of rich Burmese curries that it's easy to imagine this drink making inroads in Myanmar.

This recipe is really two drinks in one. The hibiscus water makes about 4 cups and can be cut with a little sparkling water and served over ice. Or go the next step and turn the hibiscus water into a spicy cocktail served by the pitcher. As far as spirits go, look for a good-quality blanco tequila or pisco, which also pairs well with hibiscus water. Track down dried hibiscus flowers at Mexican grocery stores.

HIBISCUS PUNCH

SERVES 8

Hibiscus Water

1 cup dried hibiscus flowers

4½ cups water

¼ cup white sugar or grated palm sugar

Handful of cilantro sprigs

½ jalapeño, sliced thinly

½ cup lime juice

3 tablespoons Ginger Juice (page 161; optional)

4 cups hibiscus water

12 ounces blanco tequila

¼ cup Palm Sugar Syrup (page 160)

Sparkling water

To make the hibiscus water, rinse the hibiscus flowers and soak for 30 minutes to an hour to soften. Drain well, put in a pot, and cover with the water. Add the sugar and bring to a gentle simmer. Cook until the flavor of the hibiscus flowers has been extracted, about 10 minutes. Let sit for 5 minutes and then strain. If the water tastes too intense for your liking, don't worry; it will be diluted later. (Alternatively, you can make it more intense by letting it steep for 20 minutes before straining.) Refrigerate until completely chilled.

To make the punch, in a small bowl, muddle the cilantro with the jalapeño with a muddler or the end of a wooden spoon. Pour in the lime juice and ginger juice, swirl the bowl, and pour the contents of the bowl into a pitcher. Pour in the hibiscus water, tequila, and sugar syrup and stir thoroughly. Chill for at least 30 minutes or overnight.

To serve, fill 8 glasses with ice. Give the pitcher a stir, pour into the glasses, and then top each glass off with sparkling water as desired.

Located in the middle of all of the cool things associated with Oakland's Temescal neighborhood, the Telegraph Avenue Burma Superstar's bar is busy enough for two bartenders to work behind but laid-back enough that no one would dare call themselves a mixologist. Since nearly everyone who sits at the bar is also there for a meal, the most important element of each cocktail is to ensure it plays well with food. This cocktail is a tribute to this dynamic. With juiced cucumber, ginger, and lime, the cocktail is essentially a refresh of a classic gin and tonic.

To make cucumber strips, peel the cucumber with a vegetable peeler. To make cucumber juice, grate a 2-ounce piece of cucumber into a bowl with a box grater or a microplane. Press the cucumber pulp through a fine-mesh strainer into another bowl.

THE TEMESCAL

MAKES 1 COCKTAIL

1 to 2 thin strips cucumber

1½ ounces gin

¾ ounce lime juice

½ ounce cucumber juice (see above)

¼ ounce Ginger Juice (page 161)

½ ounce Palm Sugar Syrup (page 160)

Tonic water

Fill a glass with cucumber strips and a handful of ice.

In a cocktail shaker, combine the gin, lime juice, cucumber juice, ginger juice, and sugar syrup. Add ice and shake. Strain into the prepared glass and top with tonic water.

REDEFINING BURMESE BEER

It doesn't take long to figure out the main beer of Myanmar. The country's namesake brew, Myanmar Beer, is a mild lager-style beer with a patriotic green, red, and yellow label. When it's blazing hot and you're looking for something cold to wash down a meal of curries, vegetables, and rice, a beer (poured over ice) is exactly what you want to drink.

Amidst America's craft beer revival, though, we're spoiled with choices. In 2013, Burma Superstar started stepping up its beer game. Osama Asif, a former manager of the Oakland restaurant, began looking for brewers who could craft a new house beer that captured the spirit of a Burmese beer without being too literal. That's when he met Morgan Cox and Steve Lopas from Ale Industries. Steve started out years ago as a home brewer before approaching Morgan, a professional brewer, about working together. To test how serious Steve was, Morgan threw a squeegee at him. The explanation: Half of the job of making craft beer is cleaning up.

They started Ale Industries in Concord, a city east of Oakland in Contra Costa County, but they outgrew their space. A century-old warehouse space once used to manufacture steel drums became available near Oakland's Fruitvale BART station, and they moved brewing operations. The brewery started doing poetry readings, jazz, and other events for the neighborhood art community. Meanwhile, Steve and Morgan set up the brewery's biofuel boiler and delivery trucks to run on recycled frying oil—some of which they pick up from Burma Superstar.

While the brewhouse makes a range of styles, Ale Industries' best-known beer is its Golden State of Mind, a lower-alcohol, hop-free beer first released in 2009 when the California beer market was saturated with West Coast IPAs. They describe it as a "tea beer," since it's gently flavored with an herbal tea made from chamomile, orange peel, and "fresh coriander" (cilantro). For the restaurant's Burma Ale beer, Steve and Morgan tweaked their tea beer, sampling ingredients such as palm sugar, tamarind, cardamom, and turmeric to see what worked the best. In the end, adding lemongrass and ginger to the existing herbal tea mix made everyone happy. After a few renditions, Burma Superstar had a Burmese beer as interpreted by an Oakland craft brewery.

After a sweltering day of temple gazing in Bagan, finding a spot to down this refreshing shandy would be heaven. (Burmese hoteliers can take this as a hint.) At Burma Superstar, Burma Ale (see sidebar, page 169) is the beer of choice for making this drink, but a lighter, not-very-hoppy beer, like Singha, works fine too. On a hot day, make a pitcher and serve it Burmese-style—over ice.

In a chilled glass, combine the ginger juice, sugar syrup, and lemon juice. Top off with beer and garnish with the orange peel.

BURMA COOLER

MAKES 1 COCKTAIL

½ ounce Ginger Juice (page 161)

¾ ounce Palm Sugar Syrup (page 160)

¾ ounce lemon or lime juice

----

12 ounces chilled unhopped beer

----

1 strip orange rind peeled with a vegetable peeler (optional)

SNACKS AND SWEETS

Go just about anywhere in Myanmar and you'll find someone selling snacks. It's an extreme kind of pop-up restaurant culture, where all it takes to get started is a spot on the side of the road, equipment to start up a fire, and a wok.

In the morning, people line up in front of vendors making fritters—Burmese tempura, some call it—to put on top of their bowls of *mohinga*. In the late afternoon, people start to line up again to eat a snack on their way home from work.

In Mandalay, Myo Naing Oo—who studied hospitality in the United Kingdom—decided to gather some of the country's best street-snack foods and sell them at his upscale restaurant MinGaLaBar, which he opened in November 2014. From 3:00 p.m. until just before dinner, the restaurant turns to tea and snacks, offering regional favorites from coconut agar-agar and semolina cake to steamed banana blossoms and sticky rice served every which way. It's an impressive display of the breadth of Burmese nibbles.

While we like to categorize these kinds of foods as appetizers or desserts in the States, in Myanmar, sweets and snacks can be eaten at any time of day—and during any part of a meal. That's why this chapter combines them. It's not unusual to have a cup of tapioca pearls and palm sugar over ice served alongside fish curry. Tea shops, where people go for their fix of Myanmar Tea (page 162), are also major places for snacking, and are evolving into places for eating full meals. At Burma Superstar, one of the most addictive snacks on the menu—*platha*—is also served at many good tea shops. A rich, buttery flatbread, platha can be made savory or sweet. For best results, pair the treats in this chapter with a drink from the previous one.

Lotus root—the stem of the lotus plant—looks like sausage links when whole and lace doilies when sliced. Because of its high starch content, this vegetable makes a good alternative to potato for frying into chips. You can get as creative as you'd like when seasoning these chips. Tamarind salt is good, but so is Japanese *furikake* or Mexican chile salt seasoning. Lotus root can also be sliced slightly thicker and added to brothy soups, such as Sour Leaf Soup (page 109), for texture. When buying lotus root, look for a whole root that feels firm. For this recipe, avoid presliced lotus root found in vacuum-sealed bags (it will be hard to slice up thinner). To ensure thin, even slices for this recipe, use a mandoline. A Japanese Benriner slicer is dependable and inexpensive.

LOTUS ROOT CHIPS

MAKES 8 TO 10 CUPS

12 ounces lotus root (about one 5-inch segment)

1½ cups canola oil

Salt or Tamarind Salt (page 217)

Peel the lotus root and slice crosswise into nearly paper-thin strips. Soak for 10 minutes in water. Drain the slices and spread on a kitchen towel to wick away excess water.

Line a baking sheet with paper towels. Have a spider or slotted spoon handy.

Heat the oil in a wok over medium-high heat. To test if the oil is hot enough, add one lotus root slice. If bubbles form around the slice right away, the oil is ready for frying. Fry the lotus root chips in batches (overcrowding the wok will cause the chips to stick together), stirring often, until golden, 3 to 4 minutes. Lower the heat if chips start turning dark brown in spots but still look raw.

Lift the chips out of the oil with the spider and scatter on the paper towels. Season with salt and repeat with the remaining chips. The chips will crisp up as they cool. Store in an air-tight container for up to 5 days.

PLATHA MAN

At night in the office above the Oakland restaurant, Har San makes the dough for *platha*, an insanely good buttery flatbread. It's a perfect setup: he has plenty of room to spread out on the stainless steel table, turn on the TV, and watch Burmese soaps while he works.

Har San was born in a village in Mon State, southeast of Yangon. His parents are farmers, and growing up, he and his siblings ate what they grew. "If you wanted beef, you had to kill a cow," he says. Har San is Muslim, and every so often his local mosque would hold a feast, killing a cow and cooking it for the whole village.

When he left Myanmar to seek job opportunities, he ended up in Chiang Mai, Thailand, where he learned how to make platha, a buttery multilayered flatbread cooked on a griddle. Chiang Mai is also where he met his wife, Rahima (see her recipe for Sour Leaf with Bamboo and Shrimp on page 51). After they were married, Rahima returned to the refugee camp on the Thai-Myanmar border where she grew up. The plan was to gain refugee status in order to eventually come to the United States. Har San stayed put selling platha until the local police shut down his operation and sent him to Rahima's camp. The couple lived there for three years before being resettled to Oakland in 2007 with the help of the International Rescue Committee. Har San estimates he had about seven years' experience making platha before coming to the States.

In Oakland, Har San's platha skills weren't being used until someone told Tiyo Bestia about him. At the time, Tiyo was the Oakland and Alameda restaurants' general manager, and she was on the lookout for skilled cooks from Myanmar. She invited Har San to come in and demonstrate what he could do, and he showed up to the interview with his entire family. The next day, he had a job.

Making platha the traditional way—with a quick throwing motion that stretches a piece of dough into one thin sheet—takes about a month to learn, he says. He first mixes the dough in a large bowl by hand (he tried using a mixer once but didn't think it worked as well). He makes a bulk batch, divides it into balls, and then dredges the balls in a mix of butter and oil. He stretches the dough into a translucent sheet, drizzles it with more butter and oil, and then folds it up so it's ready to be griddled at the restaurants.

The recipe on page 181 has been modified so that you don't need four weeks of practice before making platha. However, for those ambitious types, here's how Har San shapes each flatbread: Flatten the ball of dough into an 8-inch round. With your dominant hand, palm facing up, gently lift the edge of the dough and pinch it slightly between the lower inside part of your thumb and your palm (not with your fingertips). Gently pick up the other side with the other hand, palm facing up. In a smooth, quick motion, move your dominant hand over your other hand and then move it back so the dough is being flipped over, stretched, and flipped over again in one fast, smooth motion. Gently pull and shape the dough into a very thin, square-ish layer. Now it's ready to be drizzled with butter and oil and folded up.

With its buttery layers, this flatbread—also called *paratha* and *roti*—is the Asian answer to the croissant. The great part is how low-tech it is: you can do everything with your hands, no mixer or oven required. Feel free to practice the professional technique (see page 178) or simply follow this modified method for home cooks. If using the professional technique, consider shaping the dough into 4 portions instead of 5 to give you larger pieces of dough to stretch.

Burma Superstar serves platha with Coconut Chicken Curry (page 26), but in Burmese teahouses, it's also common to eat the bread as a breakfast treat or sweet snack. To do this, right before heating up the griddle, flatten a round of dough, add mashed banana, and then fold the dough over and seal the edges. Once the pastry has been griddled, sprinkle sugar or drizzle a little condensed milk over the top if desired.

PLATHA

MAKES 5 FLATBREADS

2 cups all-purpose flour

2 tablespoons sugar

1½ teaspoons salt

¾ cup plus 2 tablespoons lukewarm water

2 ounces unsalted butter, melted

2 tablespoons canola oil

Before you start, have ready 2 large mixing bowls and a large cast-iron pan or griddle (a well-seasoned wok works too).

In a large bowl that offers room for mixing the dough with your hands, combine the flour, sugar, and salt. Pour in ¾ cup of the water.

Using a circular motion, mix the water into the flour until a tacky mass forms. Then pull it into pieces: pluck golf ball–size pieces of dough from the mass (still keeping everything in the bowl) until the mass has been completely picked into pieces of dough. Punch the dough down a few times with your fists to knead it and bring it together. Repeat one or two more times. (This helps develop the elasticity of the dough).

Drizzle the remaining 2 tablespoons of water over the dough. Knead in the water by squishing the dough with your hands and punching it down. Once the water is incorporated, the dough should stick to your hands. If it is dry, knead in more water. Cover the bowl with plastic wrap and let rest for 20 to 50 minutes. The dough should feel soft and squishy through the plastic wrap.

Put the melted butter and oil into a separate large bowl.

Uncover the dough and pull into 5 pieces roughly 3 ounces each. Shape the pieces into balls and put them in the bowl with the melted butter, coating them on all sides. Cover the dough and let rest for 30 minutes. Keep the bowl in a place warm enough that

CONTINUED

the butter won't solidify. (If it does, fill another large bowl with hot water and place the bowl in the water to remelt the butter.)

Butter your palms with the butter from the bowl and smear a layer of butter on a work surface, preferably one that is not wood (which will absorb the oil). Put the balls on the surface.

For each ball, using your fingertips, start at the edges and pat the dough into an 8-inch round. Lift the edges of the dough with your fingertips and pull it gently toward you, shaking the dough up and down so it slaps against the surface as you stretch it. Stretch all sides of the dough this same way until you form a very thin square-ish shape about 14 inches across (or more). The dough should be thin enough that it is mostly translucent, like a foggy window. (It's okay if you have a couple of holes in the dough.) In places that are thick, spot-stretch it with your hands. If the dough resists stretching, work on another piece of the dough and come back to the stubborn one later. This lets the gluten in the dough relax a bit. If the dough folds on top of itself, simply pull the folds apart.

Once the dough is stretched out, dip your fingertips in the butter from the bowl and smear it across the dough. Fold one long side into the center of the platha. Drizzle lightly with more butter and oil. Fold the other side over until you have a long strip of folded dough. Then fold the dough in half again and again until you have an imperfect ball of dough. (If air pockets form, that's a good thing.)

Tuck the edges under to create more of an even ball and let the dough rest 20 minutes. Alternatively, place the dough in an oiled container. At this point, the platha can be refrigerated to be cooked later that day or up to 3 days later, or frozen for 1 month. (Defrost the dough overnight).

To cook the platha, flatten the ball of dough into a disk about 10 inches wide. Heat a large cast-iron griddle or skillet over medium heat. Once a drop of water sizzles on contact, put the platha in the pan and cook until evenly browned and golden in parts, 2 to 3 minutes. Flip over and continue to cook until golden brown on the other side and cooked through in the center, about 3 minutes more. Serve whole or cut into wedges.

Street vendors in Myanmar are expert fryers. These so-called tempura experts make it look easy, but in truth, frying requires practice, especially when making these crackers, a classic topping for Mohinga (page 115 and 118). The best tool for this job is a small, shallow perforated ladle (a smaller version of what's pictured on page 175), which is easy to find at Asian grocery stores. The ladle allows you to scoop up the yellow split peas while shaking off excess batter. (You only really need enough batter to hold the split peas together, no more.) Otherwise, use a regular ladle or a spoon but drain off extra batter before pouring the split peas into the oil. For the crispiest crackers, don't skimp on the amount of frying oil. Serve with mohinga or as a snack with Tamarind Ginger Dressing (page 219).

YELLOW SPLIT PEA CRACKERS

MAKES 8 TO 10 CRACKERS

½ cup yellow split peas

¼ cup rice flour

3 tablespoons chickpea flour

¼ teaspoon salt, plus more for seasoning

½ cup water

1½ cups canola oil

Cover the split peas with about 1 inch of water. Soak at least 4 hours or overnight.

Drain the split peas through a fine-mesh strainer, shaking off the excess water.

In a bowl, combine the flours and salt. Stir in the water to create a loose batter. Add the split peas and mix well. The batter will look thin, and that's a good thing: it should only lightly coat the split peas.

Line a plate with paper towels. In a wok or large skillet, heat the oil over medium-high heat. When the oil is hot but before it starts to smoke, begin frying the crackers.

Give the batter a good stir. In batches of 2 or 3, gently drop 1½ to 2 tablespoonfuls of batter into the wok for each cracker. To help the batter hold its shape, it helps to gently pour in the batter close to the surface of the oil. The fritters should spread out in the oil like silver dollar pancakes and be about 3 inches wide. Fry the crackers until they are light golden brown, about 2 minutes, nudging them a bit at the beginning to prevent them from sticking the bottom of the wok. Using a spider or metal spatula, flip the crackers over and fry about 2 minutes more or until both sides are golden brown and crispy.

Transfer the crackers to the paper towels and season with a pinch of salt. Repeat with the remaining batter, adding more oil if needed or running a perforated ladle through the oil to clean up extra bits of batter between batches. Crackers are best the day they are made, but they will keep in an airtight container at room temperature for up to 1 week.

Think of Shan Tofu as the polenta of the Burmese kitchen. It is made in a similar way (cooked in a pot with water) and can be sliced up and fried once cooled. This basic home-style recipe from Myanmar's Shan State has become so popular that you now see it all over the country. Burma Superstar has its own take (see Fried Yellow Bean Tofu, page 187), but this recipe is the old-school version. It's perfect in Shan Tofu Salad (page 139), but it also fries well and is great as a snack eaten with Tamarind Ginger Dressing (page 219). You can deep-fry it in a wok, but it also crisps up nicely when seared with a little oil in a nonstick pan.

SHAN TOFU

MAKES ONE 8 BY 4-INCH BLOCK; SERVES 8

1 cup chickpea flour

1 teaspoon salt

Scant ½ teaspoon turmeric

3 cups water

Lightly oil an 8 by 4-inch loaf pan or a similar-sized food storage container.

Whisk the flour, salt, turmeric, and 1 cup of the water. Let rest 10 minutes.

Transfer the chickpea mixture to a 4-quart pot. Over low heat, whisk in the remaining 2 cups water and cook, stirring often with a wooden spoon (preferably one with a straight side to scrape the bottom of the pot), until the puree is chunky and about as thick as Play-Doh (and similar in texture when you touch it), 5 to 8 minutes. It will also leave a film on the bottom of the pot.

Pour into the oiled pan and flatten as best as possible. (It's okay if the top isn't smooth, but a small oiled offset spatula can help spread it out.) Let cool for at least 30 minutes at room temperature before making Shan Tofu Salad. Once set, unmold the tofu and slice it in half lengthwise. Slice each rectangle crosswise into thin strips if using in a salad or into ½-inch pieces if frying (follow the instructions for frying yellow bean tofu on page 187). Alternatively, refrigerate for up to 5 days.

In this less traditional version of Shan tofu, yellow split peas lend texture while cornstarch and wheat starch help hold it together, especially when it's frying. (Wheat starch is available at Asian grocery stores, and it helps smooth out the texture of the tofu. You can skip it, but be prepared for a chunkier texture.)

Once the tofu has cooled and set, you can slice it and fry it. Tamarind Ginger Dressing (page 219), Sweet Chile Sauce (page 220), or any kind of ginger-soy sauce are also great with the tofu. Extra fried pieces can be diced and mixed into Rainbow Salad (page 95) or Superstar Vegetarian Noodles (page 92) in place of the regular soybean tofu.

FRIED YELLOW BEAN TOFU

MAKES ONE 8 BY 4-INCH BLOCK; SERVES 8

½ cup yellow split peas

2 cups water

⅓ cup chickpea flour

⅓ cup cornstarch

2 tablespoons wheat starch

1 teaspoon salt

½ teaspoon turmeric

1½ cups canola oil

Tamarind Ginger Dressing (page 219), for dipping

Cover the split peas with about 1 inch of water. Soak for at least 4 hours or overnight. Drain the split peas through a fine-mesh strainer, shaking off the excess water.

Lightly oil an 8 by 4-inch loaf pan or a similar-sized food storage container.

In a blender or food processor, blend the split peas and 1 cup of the water. Blend thoroughly for a few minutes until it's as smooth as you can make it. Blend in the flour, cornstarch, wheat starch, salt, and turmeric.

Transfer the puree to a 4-quart saucepan and whisk in the remaining 1 cup of water. Cook over medium-low heat, stirring often with a wooden spoon (preferably one with a straight side to scrape the bottom of the pot), until the puree is about as thick as Play-Doh (and similar in texture when you touch it), 5 to 8 minutes. It will also leave a film on the bottom of the pot.

Pour into the oiled pan and flatten as best as possible. (It's okay if the top isn't smooth, but a small oiled offset spatula can help spread it out.) Let cool for 20 minutes at room temperature and then refrigerate until set, about 1 hour.

Once the tofu is set, unmold it and slice it in half lengthwise. Slice each rectangle crosswise into ½-inch pieces.

Line a plate with paper towels. In a wok or large skillet, heat the oil over medium-high heat. When the oil is hot but before it starts to smoke, fry the tofu pieces in batches until golden brown, about 2 minutes per side. Using a spider or slotted spoon, transfer the tofu to the paper towels and season with a pinch of salt. Serve hot with tamarind ginger dressing.

Samosas have long been favorite Burmese tea shop snacks. There, they are served with a lime wedge alongside tea or with a tangy dip; Sweet Chile Sauce (page 220) and Tamarind Ginger Dressing (page 219) are good candidates. Samosas are also often torn into pieces and added to soup or sliced and mixed into a salad (see Samusa Salad, page 137)—more evidence that in Myanmar, anything can be turned into a salad.

There's no question that making samosas takes some time and planning, but one recipe makes a lot, and they freeze well. Make a bunch and freeze some for Samusa Soup (page 106). Or make half a recipe. To spread out the workload, make the filling the day before and refrigerate. Bring it to room temperature before shaping the samosas. Spring roll and *lumpia* wrappers come in slightly different sizes. If the squares are smaller than 6 inches, use a bit less filling. Most packets contain 25 wrappers, but some contain 20. If you have leftover potato filling, warm it up and serve it as a side dish or mix it into Samusa Soup for a thicker broth. An alternative to frying samosas is to bake them. It yields a chewier result, but for the purposes of Samusa Soup, it isn't that noticeable. To bake them, brush both sides of the samosas with oil and bake at 400°F for 10 minutes. Turn the samosas over and bake for another 10 minutes or until golden brown.

SAMOSAS

MAKES 25

2 large Yukon gold potatoes (about 1¼ pounds), peeled and cut into chunks

----

1 tablespoon canola oil, plus more for frying

½ cup minced yellow onion

½ jalapeño, minced

½ cup frozen peas

----

2 tablespoons minced cilantro

----

1 tablespoon minced mint

In a small pot, cover the potatoes with water and bring to a boil. Decrease the heat to medium-low and cook until tender when pierced with a fork, 15 to 20 minutes.

Strain the potatoes and return to the pot. Using a fork or a potato masher, mash the potatoes coarsely (you don't want them to be smooth).

In a small saucepan, heat 1 tablespoon of oil over medium-high heat. Add the onions and jalapeño and cook, stirring often, until the water has evaporated and the onions are translucent, about 3 minutes. Add the onions and jalapeños to the potatoes along with the peas, cilantro, mint, salt, turmeric, and garam masala and stir to incorporate. If the potatoes are still on the warm side, let the mixture cool to room temperature. (Alternatively, refrigerate for assembly the next day. Let it come to room temperature before using.) You will have about 4 cups, which is a little more than you'll need.

CONTINUED

1 teaspoon salt

¼ teaspoon turmeric

½ teaspoon Garam Masala (page 216)

2 tablespoons all-purpose flour

2 tablespoons water

25 large 6- to 7-inch-square spring roll or lumpia wrappers (see page 239)

2½ cups canola oil

Whisk the flour and water together in a small bowl. Have a damp towel handy for wiping off messy hands.

Separate one wrapper from the package and keep the remaining in the package to prevent them from drying out.

To shape each samosa, dip your finger into the flour and water and dampen the wrapper in three horizontal lines: along the top edge, across the center, and along the bottom edge. Fold the bottom edge over the top edge and seal to form a rectangle. Put your finger in the center of the bottom edge of the rectangle. Keeping that finger in place, fold the right side up so that it forms a 60-degree angle with the bottom edge.

Dampen under the edge and press to adhere. Fold the left side completely over to form a flattened cone, making sure that the point of the cone does not have a hole. Dampen those edges and press to adhere them. Check your work by opening up the cone and checking for gaps.

To fill, spoon about 1 heaping tablespoon of the filling into the cone. Make a gap between the filling and the wrapper. Tuck the flaps into the gap and then press to seal the edges, dampening the edges if needed.

To fry the samosas, in a wok or 4-quart pot, heat a generous inch of oil (about 2½ cups) over high heat. Line a baking sheet with paper towels. To test if the oil is hot enough, hold the edge of a samosa in the oil and see if bubbles quickly form on the surface.

In batches of 5, deep-fry the samosas, turning the heat to medium-low within the first 30 seconds of frying, until deeply golden brown, 8 to 10 minutes. Turn the samosas over frequently and baste the tops so they brown evenly. If they brown rapidly within the first 2 minutes, the oil is too hot. Turn the heat off for a few seconds and then turn it back on.

Transfer to the baking sheet to drain and season with salt as they cool. Before frying the remaining samosas, cut one fried samosa in half to see if the samosa wrapper is completely fried.

Cooled samosas can be frozen for up to 1 month and reheated in a 350°F oven until hot in the center, about 15 minutes.

Along with the samosas, these fritters go into Samusa Soup (page 106). While they are actually closer to India's *moong dal vada*, the restaurant staff likes to call them falafel, which they resemble in appearance. Soak the split peas before blending them in a food processor. To add to the Samusa Soup, first break up the falafel into pieces. On their own, they're a great snack with Sweet Chile Sauce (page 220) or Tamarind Ginger Dressing (page 219).

Cover the split peas with about 1 inch water. Soak at least 4 hours or overnight.

Drain the split peas through a fine-mesh strainer, shaking off the excess water. Pulse the split peas in a food processor until they form a coarse paste. Add the cilantro, jalapeño, onion, salt, curry powder, turmeric, and garam masala and pulse just until the ingredients are incorporated. The paste should still have some texture and feel wet.

Using your palms, shape the dough into 14 two-tablespoon balls. Flatten the balls slightly. These falafel will be soft, so they don't have to be perfectly shaped.

In a wok or 4-quart pot, heat the oil over medium-high heat. Line a baking sheet with paper towels. To test if the oil is hot enough, drop a tiny amount of batter into the oil and see if it floats quickly to the surface.

In 3 batches, lower the falafel gently into the oil. Decrease the heat to medium and fry until deeply golden brown on one side, 2 to 3 minutes, nudging the falafel a bit at the beginning to prevent them from sticking to the bottom of the wok. Using a spider or slotted spoon, flip the falafel over and cook until the remaining side is deeply golden brown, 2 to 3 minutes more. Transfer to the baking sheet to drain and season with salt as they cool.

If saving falafel for a future batch of Samusa Soup, keep in mind that cooled falafel can be frozen for up to 1 month and reheated in a 350°F oven until hot in the center, about 15 minutes.

YELLOW SPLIT PEA FALAFEL

MAKES 14 SMALL FALAFEL

1 cup yellow split peas

2 handfuls cilantro, coarsely chopped

½ jalapeño, coarsely chopped

¼ cup chopped red onion or shallot

1 teaspoon salt

¾ teaspoon Madras curry powder

½ teaspoon turmeric

½ teaspoon Garam Masala (page 216)

1½ cups canola oil

There are so many ways to modify this Southeast Asian comfort-food dessert to make it yours. Skip the coconut cream and go with a big scoop of coconut ice cream if decadence is your thing. Crushed peanuts, toasted almonds, or sesame seeds, can add a bit of crunch if that's what you're after. For the rice, though, only one will do: look for deeply purple glutinous rice. It cooks more evenly when soaked overnight.

Cover the rice with about an inch of water and soak overnight.

Drain the rice through a fine-mesh strainer, shaking off the excess water. Put the rice, the 1½ cups water, and salt in a pot. Cover and bring to a boil. Once the lid starts rattling, lower to a gentle simmer and cook for 30 minutes. Remove the lid, give the pot a stir, and continue to cook with the lid off for 10 minutes.

Meanwhile, make the simple syrup. In a small saucepan, combine the ½ cup sugar and ½ cup water. Simmer over medium-low heat until the sugar has dissolved completely and the liquid has thickened enough to lightly coat a spoon, 6 to 10 minutes. Pour the sugar syrup over the cooked rice and stir with a fork. Cover the rice and let it sit for 10 more minutes.

To make the coconut cream, heat the coconut milk, the 1 tablespoon of sugar, and salt in a small high-sided pot over medium heat. As the milk heats up, it will start to splatter. To avoid too much mess, stir often and keep a towel handy. Once the milk starts bubbling, lower to a gentle simmer and cook until it has been reduced to about 1 cup and easily coats the back of a spoon, about 10 minutes.

Serve the coconut rice warm or at room temperature. Drizzle a little condensed milk in each bowl. Scoop a generous spoonful of rice in the center of the bowl and spoon the coconut cream on top. Serve with toasted sesame seeds and mangoes.

BLACK RICE PUDDING

SERVES 6 TO 8

Rice

1½ cups black sticky rice

1½ cups water

1 teaspoon salt

Simple Syrup

½ cup chopped palm sugar or white sugar

½ cup water

Coconut Cream

1 (13½-ounce) can unsweetened coconut milk

1 tablespoon grated palm sugar or white sugar

Pinch of salt

Serving (any or all of the following)

Sweetened condensed milk

Toasted sesame seeds, toasted sliced almonds, or chopped peanuts

1 mango or 2 bananas, diced

One of the most widely found desserts in Myanmar, this chewy, not-too-sweet cake is a perfect accompaniment to Myanmar Tea (page 162). Although semolina is in the name, the cake doesn't use the type of semolina flour you might be familiar with from Italian cuisine. Instead, there are two options: farina, finely ground cereal grains (and the main ingredient in Cream of Wheat), which can be found among Middle Eastern ingredients at food stores; or *suji* (also spelled *sooji*), a pale, grainy flour sold in Indian grocery stores. The traditional topping for semolina cake is white poppy seeds, which are sold in Indian and Japanese food stores. Using sliced almonds in their place (or leaving them out) is fine too. An aromatic (preferably unrefined) peanut oil gives the cake a pleasant nutty flavor, but melted butter or canola oil will also work.

SEMOLINA CAKE

MAKES 18 PIECES

1 cup farina or suji

1 cup white sugar or chopped palm sugar

¼ teaspoon salt

1 (13½-ounce) can coconut milk

1½ cups water

2 large eggs

2 tablespoons peanut oil

2 tablespoons white poppy seeds or ¼ cup sliced almonds

2 tablespoons butter

Preheat the oven to 350°F. Butter an 8 by 8-inch baking pan.

Spread the farina on a rimmed baking sheet and toast until aromatic and lightly browned, 15 minutes.

In a 3-quart (or larger) pot, whisk together the sugar, salt, coconut milk, and water. Heat over medium heat, whisking often, until the sugar has dissolved, about 4 minutes (this will take longer for palm sugar than for white sugar).

In a medium bowl, whisk together the eggs. To temper the eggs (and prevent them from scrambling), drizzle about ½ cup of the hot coconut-sugar liquid into the eggs while whisking continuously until incorporated. Whisk the egg mixture into the pot with the rest of the coconut-sugar liquid and cook, whisking continuously, for 1 minute.

Pour the farina to the egg mixture gradually, whisking well to avoid lumps. Switch to a rubber spatula or wooden spoon and cook the batter, stirring often, for 4 to 5 minutes. The batter will thicken quickly, but keep stirring until a film forms at the bottom of the pan. Stir in the oil.

Pour the batter into the prepared pan. Sprinkle the poppy seeds evenly over the top. Bake until lightly set, with the sides bubbling, about 35 minutes. Dot the butter on top and return to the oven for 5 minutes more to let the butter melt into the cake.

Let the cake cool in the pan for at least 30 minutes. Cut into 3 strips across and 6 strips down to make 18 rectangles. The cake keeps covered, at room temperature for a few days.

While desserts aren't common after a meal in Myanmar, some restaurants do serve a small plate of this coconut jelly, each piece speared with a toothpick to make for easy eating. The flavor is simple but cooling after a garlic- and chile-filled meal. The best part about the dessert is how the coconut water naturally separates from the coconut cream, creating a layered dessert. This recipe has been re-created to make the separation more dramatic, with a separate layer of coconut water and coconut flakes added for texture.

Agar-agar is a seaweed-based alternative to gelatin, but it works in a similar way. The big benefit of agar-agar over gelatin (other than its being vegan) is that it sets at room temperature. The range of agar-agar products—from flakes to powders premixed with sugar—is broad, and they are not interchangeable. For the purposes of this recipe, seek out the natural agar-agar flakes from Eden.

COCONUT AGAR JELLY

MAKES ONE 8 BY 4-INCH LOAF; SERVES 10

First Layer

1 (13½-ounce) can coconut milk

½ cup water

¼ cup sugar

¼ cup agar-agar flakes

Pinch of salt

Second Layer

1 cup coconut water

1½ tablespoons agar-agar flakes

1 teaspoon sugar

2 tablespoons dried unsweetened coconut flakes

Lightly oil an 8 by 4-inch loaf pan or a similar-sized food storage container. You can also opt to line with parchment paper so that the paper hangs over the edges of the long sides. (This can help with unmolding but is not essential.)

To make the first layer, in a 2-quart pot, whisk together the coconut milk, water, sugar, agar-agar, and salt over medium-high heat. Bring to a boil and then lower to a simmer until the agar-agar and sugar have dissolved, about 5 minutes. Keep an eye on the pot and give it a good stir if it looks like it's going to boil over.

Pour into the prepared pan and let the jelly almost set at room temperature, 45 minutes to 1 hour. (You can tap the jelly on top with your finger to see how firm it's become.)

To make the second layer, in the same pot, whisk together the coconut water, agar-agar, and sugar. Bring to a boil, then lower to a simmer and cook until the agar-agar and sugar have dissolved, about 3 minutes. Let sit for a couple of minutes and then pour over the bottom layer. Sprinkle the coconut flakes on top and let set completely, about 1 hour. If you want it to set faster, refrigerate it.

Once the jelly has set, cut it into slices. The jelly refrigerated, keeps for about 1 week.

RICE AND BASICS

Cook enough Burmese dishes and you'll develop
an understanding of its fundamentals: rice, aromatics,
vegetables, spices, crunchy bits, fish sauce
or shrimp paste, and a little protein.

In restaurant kitchens, chefs set themselves up for success by preparing a bunch of small yet important components that allow them to put together dishes quickly. This is not a new idea for Burmese home cooks, who have been doing this for years.

In Burmese kitchens, jars of toasted chickpea flour, fried onions, and fried garlic are ready to be sprinkled over all sorts of dishes, from noodles to salads. Since oil is never wasted, it's used as a flavoring agent. The oil used to fry onions or garlic is saved and drizzled over salads or noodles.

Preparing a few of these staples ahead of time makes cooking out of this book much easier, especially when it comes to salads. So make a big batch to use on several recipes. And make extra fried onions. Because you can never have too many fried onions.

This section of the book is set up in two parts. First, it shares techniques and recipes for making rice. Next, it offers all the condiments that make Burmese food crunchy, spicy, aromatic, and memorable. Flip to this section any time you need to stock up on Burmese staples.

COOKING RICE

A few notes on cooking methods: People make a big deal about cooking rice, but it is not complicated. If you have a pot and a stove, you're good to go. If using a rice cooker, you can get away with less water than if you cook rice on a stovetop. Yet rice cookers are a little trickier because each is different. Follow the instructions that come with the machine and make adjustments as needed. No matter which vessel you choose, rinse the rice a few times before cooking it until the water runs mostly clear. The key to a not-too-wet texture is letting the kernels dry out a bit before cooking. Putting the strainer over a pot, turning the heat on for a minute, and letting the rice steam slightly with the residual heat speeds up the drying process.

While coconut rice is more of a special-occasion starch in Myanmar, it's a staple at Burma Superstar. The sweet, aromatic rice is a reliable partner for Coconut Chicken Curry (page 26) and Pumpkin Pork Stew (page 33), but it can be easily dressed up for dessert with slices of mango and a drizzle of condensed milk. It is also easy to make at home in a rice cooker or in a pot. If sweetened rice isn't your thing, leave out the sugar and reduce the salt to a pinch. If you want to go all out, serve with Fried Onions (page 208) on top. For the most aromatic rice, opt for virgin coconut oil over refined coconut oil.

COCONUT RICE

FOR 4 SERVINGS

1½ cups jasmine rice

1 cup coconut milk, well-stirred if separated

1 cup water, minus 1 tablespoon if using a rice cooker

2 tablespoons white sugar or chopped palm sugar (optional)

½ teaspoon salt

1 tablespoon virgin coconut oil

FOR 6 SERVINGS

2 cups jasmine rice

1⅓ cups coconut milk, well-stirred if separated

1⅓ cups water, minus 2 tablespoons if using a rice cooker

2¼ tablespoons white sugar or chopped palm sugar (optional)

¾ teaspoon salt

2 tablespoons virgin coconut oil

Wash the rice well in fresh changes of water, draining through a fine-mesh strainer after each wash, until the water runs nearly clear, 3 to 4 washes. After the final wash, let the rice drain in the strainer for at least 15 minutes to allow the excess water to drip off. (The rice will dry faster if you place the strainer over a pot and turn the heat on for a minute.)

While the rice drains, combine the coconut milk and water in a 1-quart liquid measuring cup, using the corresponding amount of liquid for the chosen cooking method.

Stovetop Method: Empty the strainer of rice into a pot. Briefly mix in the sugar, salt, and coconut oil, taking care not to break up the kernels. Pour in the coconut milk and water. Cover the pot and bring to a boil. When the lid starts to rattle, remove the lid and give the rice a stir. Cover the pot and decrease the heat to the lowest setting. Cook for 10 minutes. Remove from the heat and let sit for 15 minutes. This allows the rice to continue to absorb the liquid. Fluff with a fork before serving.

Rice Cooker Method: Put the rice in the rice cooker. Briefly mix in the sugar, salt, and coconut oil, taking care not to break up the kernels. Pour in the coconut milk and water. Cook on the white rice setting. When the rice is finished, let it continue to steam in the cooker, ideally for 20 minutes, to allow the kernels to absorb all of the liquid. Fluff with a fork before serving.

No one in Myanmar would ever make coconut rice with brown rice, but brown rice is so popular in California that it seemed to make sense to embrace the state's healthy living ethos and create a coconut brown rice recipe for this book. Brown rice doesn't absorb coconut milk as easily as white rice, so it's necessary to use less coconut milk. The resulting rice resembles porridge, but the flavor is undeniably about coconut.

BROWN COCONUT RICE

SERVES 4 TO 5

1½ cups brown jasmine rice

1 cup coconut milk, well-stirred if separated

1¾ cups water

2 tablespoons white sugar or chopped palm sugar (optional)

½ teaspoon salt

1 tablespoon virgin coconut oil

Wash the rice well and drain through a fine-mesh strainer, letting the rice drain for at least 15 minutes to allow the excess water to drip off. (The rice will dry faster if you place the strainer over a pot and turn the heat on for a minute.)

While the rice drains, combine the coconut milk and water in a 1-quart liquid measuring cup.

Stovetop Method: Empty the strainer of rice into a pot. Briefly mix in the sugar, salt, and coconut oil. Pour in the coconut milk and water. Cover the pot and bring to a boil. When the lid starts to rattle, remove the lid and give the rice a stir. Cover the pot and decrease the heat to the lowest setting. Cook for 40 minutes. Remove from the heat and let sit for 15 minutes. This allows the rice to continue to absorb the liquid, which is especially important for brown rice. Fluff with a fork before serving.

Rice Cooker Method: Put the rice in the rice cooker. Briefly mix in the sugar, salt, and coconut oil, taking care not to break up the kernels. Pour in the coconut milk and water. Cook on the brown rice setting. When the rice is finished, let it continue to steam in the rice cooker, ideally for 20 minutes, to allow the kernels to absorb all of the liquid. Fluff with a fork before serving.

Prior to World War II, Myanmar was the number-one rice exporter in the world. While rice grows in other parts of Myanmar—the landscape between Hsipaw in the Shan State and Mandalay is dotted with patties—the best rice-growing region is the steamy, flat Ayeyarwady Delta region southwest of Yangon.

Rice is integral to nearly every meal in Myanmar too, where it's often the first thing girls are taught how to cook. Besides, eating curry without rice is crazy, no matter how anti-carb you are.

JASMINE RICE

Wash the rice well in fresh changes of water, draining through a fine-mesh strainer after each wash, until the water runs nearly clear, 3 to 4 washes. After the final wash, let the rice drain in the strainer for at least 15 minutes to allow the excess water to drip off. (The rice will dry faster if you place the strainer over a pot and turn the heat on for a minute.)

Stovetop Method: Empty the strainer of rice into a pot. Pour in the water. Cover the pot, and bring to a boil. When the lid starts to rattle, remove the lid and give the rice a stir. Cover the pot and decrease the heat to the lowest setting. Cook for 10 minutes. Remove from the heat and let sit for 15 minutes. This allows the rice to continue to absorb the liquid. Fluff with a fork before serving.

Rice Cooker Method: Put the rice and water in the rice cooker and cook on the white rice setting. When the rice is finished, let it continue to steam in the cooker for 15 minutes. This allows the rice to continue to absorb the liquid. Fluff with a fork before serving.

FOR 4 SERVINGS

1½ cups jasmine rice, minus
1 tablespoon if using a rice cooker

1¾ cups water

FOR 6 SERVINGS

2 cups jasmine rice

2⅔ cups water, minus 2 tablespoons
if using a rice cooker

Frying onions requires a decent amount of oil and some patience. The good news is that the fried onions keep well for a week or two in an airtight jar (although they lose their crispness when stored—which is perfectly okay). And all that onion frying oil comes in handy when you're making Burmese salads.

Thin, evenly sliced onions will fry more uniformly. Use a sharp chef's knife and halve through the root end. Peel the onion and trim off the root. Slice each half thinly lengthwise (from the tip to the root end), not crosswise. If you want to use shallots instead, use the same method: halve the shallots and slice lengthwise into strips (not crosswise into half-rings).

FRIED ONIONS AND ONION OIL

MAKES ABOUT 1½ CUPS FRIED ONIONS AND JUST OVER 1 CUP ONION OIL

1¼ cups canola oil

2 cups thinly sliced yellow onion

¼ teaspoon salt

Line a heatproof bowl with a strainer. Line a plate with paper towels.

In a wok or 2- to 3-quart saucepan, heat the oil over medium heat for a minute or two (the oil shouldn't be scorching hot). Add a piece of onion to test the heat of the oil—if bubbles form around the piece right away, the oil is hot enough. Fry the onion slices, stirring often. Within a minute or two, decrease the heat to low and continue to fry, stirring often, until deep golden, about 20 minutes. Be patient—the onions take a while to change color, but once they do, it happens quickly. You are close when you notice that fewer bubbles gather around the sides of the onions. If the onions are close to being done, you can turn off the oil and let them continue to cook in the hot oil for another minute or two.

Pour the contents of the saucepan into the strainer-lined bowl. Lift the strainer up and shake off the excess oil. Scatter the onion pieces onto the lined plate and season with salt. The fried onions can be stored in an airtight container at room temperature for up to 1 week or in the refrigerator for 1 month. Store the oil in the refrigerator for up to 2 months.

In Myanmar, crisp pieces of garlic are sprinkled on everything from noodles to salads to rice. Asian grocery stores often sell bits of fried garlic in jars—and there's no shame in buying them to save the step—but it's not hard to make them yourself. Just thinly slice garlic and then gently fry it in oil until golden.

Dehydrated garlic chips sold in Chinese grocery stores are another way to go. They retain their crunchy texture for a longer period of time once fried. They first need to be rehydrated in cool water and then fried gently so they don't turn bitter. Follow the prompts in the recipe for the garlic type you are using. No matter what kind of garlic, store the remaining oil in the refrigerator to use in recipes such as Garlic Noodles (page 101) or in salads in place of onion frying oil or canola oil.

FRIED GARLIC CHIPS AND GARLIC OIL

MAKES ABOUT ⅓ CUP FRIED GARLIC AND ABOUT ½ CUP GARLIC OIL

⅓ cup thinly sliced fresh garlic or dehydrated garlic chips

½ cup canola oil

If using dehydrated garlic chips, soak them in cold water for 4 minutes. Drain and let sit for 15 minutes to allow the centers of the chips to hydrate.

Line a heatproof bowl with a strainer. Line a plate with paper towels.

In a wok or small saucepan, heat the oil over medium heat for a minute or two (the oil shouldn't be scorching hot). Add the garlic and gently stir into the oil. When bubbles start to form rapidly around the garlic, decrease the heat to low and cook, stirring often, until the garlic is an even golden color and nearly completely crisp, about 3 minutes if using fresh garlic and 7 minutes if using dehydrated garlic chips. If the garlic starts to darken too quickly, remove it from the heat and let it continue to fry in the oil. If the garlic needs more time to fry, return the wok to low heat and continue to fry.

Pour the contents of the wok into the strainer-lined bowl. Lift the strainer up and shake off the excess oil. Scatter the garlic onto the lined plate. The garlic should crisp up as it cools. The chips can be stored in an airtight container at room temperature for 1 month. Store the oil in the refrigerator for up to 6 months.

There are few Burmese meals that aren't improved by the onion/garlic/dried shrimp mixture that constitutes *ngapi kyaw*, or, as some call it, *balachaung*. It's the crispy cousin of Tomato Shrimp Relish with Grilled Okra (page 48). Sprinkle a spoonful over broccoli, water spinach, or cauliflower or pile it on top of deep-fried fish. It's an easy way to dress up plain jasmine rice too. Dried shrimp (see page 235) creates a natural MSG effect, but even if you leave the shrimp out to make a vegetarian version, you will still have a deeply flavorful condiment on your hands. Use the leftover cooking oil in any recipe that calls for onion frying oil.

NGAPI KYAW

MAKES ABOUT 1½ CUPS

½ cup dried shrimp

1 cup canola oil

2 cups sliced onion

⅓ cup garlic cloves, thinly sliced

½ teaspoon dried chile flakes

¼ teaspoon salt

In a food processor or a coffee grinder reserved for grinding spices, grind the shrimp into a fine powder. This may take a few minutes, especially if the shrimp have been stored in the freezer. (To clean the coffee grinder afterward, grind uncooked white rice in it.)

Line a heatproof bowl with a strainer.

In a wok or 2- to 3-quart saucepan, heat the oil over medium heat for a minute or two (the oil shouldn't be scorching hot). Add a piece of onion to test the heat of the oil—if bubbles form around the edge's right away, the oil is hot enough.

Fry the onion slices, stirring often to promote even frying. Within a minute or two, decrease the heat to medium-low and continue to fry, stirring often, until the onions are golden and starting to brown in spots, about 12 minutes.

Add the garlic and cook until golden and crisp, about 3 minutes. Turn off the heat and add the chile flakes, allowing the chile flakes to steep into the oil for 1 minute. (For a spicier version, add more chile flakes.)

Pour the contents of the wok into the strainer-lined bowl. Lift the strainer up and shake off the excess oil. Return the onions and garlic to the wok and heat the wok to medium. Add the shrimp powder and mix it into the onions and garlic. Season with salt and gently toast the mixture for about 2 minutes. Transfer to a bowl and let cool to room temperature.

The condiment can be stored in an airtight container at room temperature for up to 5 days or in the refrigerator for 1 month.

A Burmese meal never seems complete without the addition of crunchy fried split peas or nuts. Yellow split peas look quite similar to *chana dal*—split baby chickpeas—but they are slightly flatter. It is crucial to soak split peas overnight before frying them to soften them and prepare them to take in oil. To soften the split peas more thoroughly as they soak in water, you can also add a pinch of baking soda.

Cover the split peas with about 1 inch of water. Soak at least 4 hours or overnight.

Drain the split peas through a fine-mesh strainer, shaking off the excess water.

Line a plate with paper towels. In a wok or small saucepan, heat the oil over medium-high heat for 1 minute. Add the split peas. Once the oil starts to bubble rapidly around the split peas, lower the heat slightly and continue to fry, stirring often, until they begin to crisp up and turn slightly darker, about 5 minutes.

Drain well. Scatter the split peas on the lined plate and season with salt. The split peas should be crunchy but not rock-hard once cooled. They can be stored in an airtight container at room temperature for 2 weeks.

FRIED YELLOW SPLIT PEAS

MAKES ABOUT ½ CUP

⅓ cup yellow split peas

½ cup canola oil

Pinch of salt

Since the recipes in this book that require mustard and cumin seeds have the toasting and grinding steps built in, you don't necessarily need to make this spice blend. But if you really like the flavors of Chili Lamb (page 86) or Samusa Soup (page 106), it's not a bad idea to make a batch to cut out work down the road, especially if you have a couple of large bags of spices from an Indian market. The spice blend is also great tossed into any of the kebats (page 81 to 85) or a simple bowl of lentils.

In a dry wok or skillet, toast the cumin and mustard seeds until the cumin is fragrant and the mustard seeds start to pop, no more than 30 seconds. Transfer to a mortar with a pestle, or a coffee grinder used for grinding spices, and pulverize to a coarse powder. Store in a sealed container at cool room temperature for up to 4 months.

MUSTARD-CUMIN SPICE BLEND

MAKES ½ CUP

¼ cup cumin seeds
- -
¼ cup black mustard seeds
- -

TOASTED CHICKPEA FLOUR

Chickpea flour is always toasted before it's mixed into Burmese salads and noodle dishes. Toasted chickpea flour keeps in an airtight container at room temperature for up to 2 months. For longer storage, keep it in the freezer.

For a small batch, spread ¼ cup of flour in a skillet and heat over medium heat, stirring often, for 3 to 4 minutes or until the flour has deepened to a light caramel color.

For larger batches, use the oven. Heat the oven to 350°F. Spread 1 cup of flour across a rimmed baking pan. Bake, stirring often, until the edges are starting to brown and the center is a light caramel color, about 20 minutes. The toasted flour keeps for a few months in a cool, dark place, making it convenient to have on hand for sprinkling on salads and noodle dishes.

A pinch of garam masala in curries is another way that Burmese kitchens pay tribute to Indian influences. While the spice blend is used sparingly in other parts of the country, it is common in Yangon. You can buy premade garam masala for the recipes in this book, but it's not hard to make your own with a coffee grinder used for grinding spices. If buying garam masala, look for small packets for optimal freshness. Spicely stores or online are a reliable option.

GARAM MASALA

MAKES ¼ CUP

15 green cardamom pods

1 to 2 cinnamon sticks

12 cloves

1 tablespoon coriander seeds

2 teaspoons cumin seeds

2 teaspoons black peppercorns

1 teaspoon fennel seeds

Crush the cardamom lightly and remove the outer green pod. Crush the cinnamon sticks using the bottom of a skillet or a mortar with a pestle.

Add all the spices to a dry skillet and heat over medium heat, stirring frequently, until fragrant, about 2 minutes. Watch the spices carefully to ensure they don't darken. Let the spices cool to warm room temperature. (If the spices are browning in the pan after you turned off the heat, pour them into a bowl to stop the toasting.)

Pour the spices into a coffee grinder used for grinding spices and pulse several times until the spice blend is uniform and no large pieces of cinnamon remain. Store in an airtight container for up to 3 months.

Because tamarind and salt both make your mouth water, think of this as a home-made MSG substitute. It can be used on virtually everything in this book that needs more salt. A coffee grinder reserved for spices is all you need to make tamarind salt, although the machine will get a bit of a workout. Tamarind salt is also a great alternative to fish sauce if you're looking to keep things on the vegetarian side—it's the perfect seasoning for Pumpkin Tofu Stew (page 35).

Pull the tamarind pulp into small pieces with your hands, removing any large pits. Toss the pulp in the salt and let it dry out for at least an hour or overnight. In two batches, pulse the salt and tamarind in a coffee grinder until the tamarind is ground thoroughly into the salt. Be patient. If the grinder gets jammed, give it a shake and try grinding again.

Store in an airtight container indefinitely.

TAMARIND SALT

MAKES A HEAPING ¼ CUP

¾ ounce seedless tamarind pulp
(see page 238)

½ cup salt

Think of this condiment as an alternative to lime juice. In traditional Burmese fish curries and soups, tamarind water—not citrus—is what brightens flavors. Freeze extra to save for the dressing for Rainbow Salad (page 95) or for making Sour Leaf Soup (page 109) or Home-Style Shrimp Kebat (page 84). You can even serve it in a bowl with a small spoon for seasoning dishes, like Pork Curry with Green Mango Pickle (page 36), at the table. See page 238 for information on buying tamarind pulp.

TAMARIND WATER

MAKES ABOUT ⅔ CUP

¾ cup hot water

- -

1½ ounces seedless tamarind pulp

- -

In a bowl, pour the water over the tamarind and let it soak for 5 to 10 minutes, occasionally using your hands or a spoon to squish the pulp and help it dissolve into the water.

Strain through a fine-mesh strainer, pressing down on the pulp to extract more tamarind paste. The water tends to settle, with some of the tamarind solids falling to the bottom of the container. Stir before using.

Tamarind water keeps for 1 week in the refrigerator and 6 months in the freezer.

Compared with straight-up tamarind water, this recipe uses a more concentrated amount of tamarind pulp. This dressing does double-duty as a dipping sauce for samosas and falafels as well as a dressing for Samusa Salad (page 137). Grating ginger with a microplane gives the sauce a more potent ginger flavor, but minced does the job too. See page 238 for information on buying tamarind pulp.

In a bowl, pour the water over the tamarind and let it soak for 5 to 10 minutes, occasionally using your hands or a spoon to squish the pulp and help it dissolve into the water.

Strain through a fine-mesh strainer, pressing down on the pulp to extract more tamarind paste. The water tends to settle, with some of the tamarind solids falling to the bottom of the container.

Mix in the ginger, garlic, sugar, and salt. Taste, adjusting sugar and salt if needed. If the sauce is too thick or tastes too sour, add a splash of water to thin it slightly.

The dressing keeps for 1 week in the refrigerator.

TAMARIND GINGER DRESSING

MAKES ABOUT 1 CUP

¾ cup hot water

2½ ounces seedless tamarind pulp

1 teaspoon grated ginger

1 teaspoon minced garlic

1 teaspoon sugar

½ teaspoon salt

This sauce comes together in minutes and is essentially a simple way to doctor up the bottle of sriracha that you probably already have in the refrigerator. Add it to noodles (it's great with Garlic Noodles, page 101) or use it as a dip for Samosas (page 188).

SWEET CHILE SAUCE

Mix everything together and use immediately or refrigerate and use within 5 days.

MAKES ABOUT ½ CUP

½ cup sriracha

2 tablespoons minced jalapeño

2 tablespoons minced shallot or red onion

1 tablespoon sugar

1 tablespoon freshly squeezed lime juice

It's always nice to have chile oil on hand to add zip to so many things, from soup and salad to fried fish and chicken curries. This one has a bonus: bits of gently fried chile flakes, which can be scooped out from the bottom and spooned on top of noodles and rice. It's easy to make chile oil with basic supermarket finds: vegetable oil and dried chile flakes. The oil isn't strained, so it gets hotter as it sits. If it becomes too hot to handle, add more oil.

In a blender or food processor, start grinding the chile flakes with 1 tablespoon oil. Gradually drizzle in up to ½ cup of oil until a chunky paste forms. Drizzle in the remaining oil.

In a small saucepan, gently heat the oil over medium-low heat until the chiles start to sizzle, about 2 minutes. Pull off the heat and let cool completely.

The oil can be stored at cool room temperature for several weeks or refrigerated indefinitely. Top off with more oil to dilute the spiciness if desired.

CHILE OIL

MAKES 1 CUP

¼ cup dried chile flakes
- -
1 cup canola oil
- -

It's easy enough to buy a decent jar of mango pickle at an Indian market or well-stocked international grocery store. Burma Superstar buys just that for making Pork Curry with Green Mango Pickle (page 36). But for those who like extra-credit projects, here's a tart homemade version that does the job nicely.

Some green mango recipes call for allowing the fruit to dry under intense sun to concentrate the flavors. Here, a low oven helps slightly dehydrate the mangoes. When buying mangoes, look for small or medium-sized fruit with smooth green skin. The best ones reach grocery stores that stock Asian produce in the spring. Green mangoes sold in the United States most often come from Central America or Mexico, and they are larger and less sour than the Indian green mangoes favored for this pickle. To compensate, squeeze lime juice over the top. This is the only recipe in the book that calls for fenugreek seeds, so buy them in a small quantity if possible—but don't leave them out. They give the mango pickle part of its distinct flavor.

GREEN MANGO PICKLE

MAKES ABOUT 1½ CUPS

2 cups chopped green mango
(from one 10- to 13-ounce mango),
unpeeled

1 tablespoon salt

1 tablespoon paprika

1 teaspoon cumin seeds

½ teaspoon turmeric

2 teaspoons fenugreek seeds

1 teaspoon black mustard seeds

2 tablespoons canola oil

2 garlic cloves, crushed with
the side of a knife

Juice of 1 lime

Preheat the oven to 200°F. On a rimmed baking sheet, mix the mango well with the salt, paprika, cumin seeds, and turmeric. Bake for 2 hours to dry out the mango, allowing the spices to infuse the mango flesh. The mango skin will start to curl in at the edges as it dries.

Transfer the mango pieces to a bowl. In a small saucepan, toast the fenugreek and mustard seeds over medium heat until aromatic, about 1 minute. Grind in a mortar with a pestle or a coffee grinder used for grinding spices and then mix into the mango.

In the same saucepan, heat the oil over medium heat. Add the garlic and cook until the cloves just start to turn golden, about 1 minute. Mix the oil and garlic into the mango. At this point, the mango will be a warm room temperature.

Transfer the mango to a glass jar. Squeeze the lime juice over the mango, cap the jar, and give it a good shake. Keep the jar out at room temperature for 2 to 3 days, giving it a shake once or twice daily, and then refrigerate. The mango pickle keeps for up to 6 months.

It's common to eat a small bowl of Chinese-style pickled mustard greens along-side Shan Noodles (page 100). In the Shan hills, the condiment is often made by drying the greens out in the sun and then fermenting them. This version is an urban pickler's shortcut. Instead of fermentation, vinegar delivers the acidity. This pickle works well with Garlic Noodles (page 101) or even served alongside rich dishes, like Pumpkin Pork Stew (page 33). Look for Chinese mustard greens, also called gai choy, at Asian grocery stores.

PICKLED MUSTARD GREENS

MAKES ABOUT 2 CUPS

6 ounces Chinese mustard greens

¾ cup distilled white vinegar

¼ cup sugar

1 tablespoon salt

1 small, dried chile, broken in half (optional)

Bring a large pot of water to a boil. Spread a kitchen towel on a rimmed baking sheet and have a spider or pair of tongs handy.

Separate the mustard leaves and give them a good wash. Boil the greens until just tender, about 1 minute and then lift them out of the water and spread them across the towel. Once the greens have cooled to room temperature, roll the towel up and squeeze to remove excess water. Coarsely chop the greens.

Meanwhile, in a pot, bring the vinegar, sugar, salt, and chile, if using, to a boil until the sugar has dissolved. Allow the brine to cool to warm room temperature.

In a bowl, mix together the greens and brine and transfer to a glass pint jar. Let the greens sit at room temperature for 1 day. The pickle keeps in the refrigerator for at least 6 months.

PANTRY, TOOLS, AND TECHNIQUES

Clockwise, from top: dried shrimp, paprika, cayenne, small dried chiles and chile flakes, dried yellow split peas, chickpea flour, peanuts and sesame seeds, tumeric, and center, dried shrimp powder.

With its bins of cumin and mustard seeds, bags of yellow split peas and jasmine rice, blocks of tamarind, and bottles of everything from sambal and fish sauce to Madras curry powder and Chinese noodles, it seems as though the Burma Superstar pantry boarded a Pan-Asian express train.

This mix of ingredients from all over Asia forms the Burma Superstar pantry. With the exception of *laphet* (fermented tea leaves; see page 143), most ingredients used in this book can be found at both specialty and general grocery stores that stock Chinese, Southeast Asian, Indian, or Latin American ingredients. The first time you buy a bag of dried shrimp or a block of tamarind pulp, it may seem tough to imagine how you will use it all up. But many of these ingredients have long shelf lives, giving you enough time to explore different ways to put them to good use—for the recipes in this book and beyond (many have crossover use in other cuisines).

The Pantry

AROMATICS AND HERBS

If you had to pick the most-used ingredients in the Burma Superstar kitchen, they would probably come from this section. It's hard to think of a dish where garlic or onions don't play key roles. Add ginger and lemongrass and you have the base of most of the curries in this book.

Cilantro The way cooks in Myanmar use cilantro is to drape big sprigs over the top of a salad or snip the leaves with a pair of scissors over a soup right before serving. Chopping up stems as well as leaves is absolutely okay. For any gardeners out there, don't get bent out of shape if your cilantro

has started flowering—just use it. Its flavor at that stage is closer to the flavor of cilantro in Myanmar.

Garlic The garlic that grows in Myanmar is small and sweet—so sweet that it's common to serve raw whole cloves alongside laphet after a meal. Whether pounded or minced, garlic is also a key seasoning agent in nearly every dish cooked with onions. Peeling garlic cloves can take a lot of time. To make faster work of the job, break up a whole head of cloves and soak them in water for a few minutes before peeling. If mincing cloves is taking too long, whirl them up in a food processor. Burmese cooks in America find no shame in using one for mincing garlic or onions.

Ginger and Galangal Ginger is by far the more frequently used fresh rhizome in this book, though galangal makes one important cameo in the Rakhine Mohinga (page 118). The two ingredients are like cousins—similar, but not mistakable for one another. Ginger is more potent and spicy, adding an unmistakable freshness to dishes. In this book, it's also juiced and used extensively in tea and cocktails. In comparison, galangal is lighter in color, with a floral, almost soapy smell. Since galangal is harder to find than ginger, mince all of it up when you find it and freeze it for future use. Peel both roots by scraping off the skin with the tip of a spoon (this removes less of the root's flesh than a vegetable peeler or paring knife).

Green Onions/Scallions Culinary students in the States used to be taught that adding GGS—ginger, garlic, and scallions—instantly makes a dish Chinese. That's not completely true, but there is some validity to it. In this book, when sliced green onions are added, it usually indicates that a dish leans Chinese. When slicing green onions, use both the white and green parts. Like raw onions or shallots, sliced green onions can be soaked in cold water to remove some of their raw bite.

Lemongrass In Burmese curries and soups, lemongrass plays a subtle role. It's often added in large pieces to make it easy to pull out, but it's minced in dishes when its flavor is meant to be more pronounced. When shopping for lemongrass, look for thick, firm stalks. Before cutting the lemongrass, chop off the tough root end and the thin, hollow top end and then peel off the outer layer. Slice the stalk in half lengthwise through the end. To tenderize the stalk so it can better release its flavor in a curry, smash it with the side of a chef's knife or cleaver. This is also good to do before mincing because it softens the stalk. If you happen to chop up more lemongrass than you need, freeze to use down the road.

Mint Add mint to give nearly any salad, curry, or stir-fry a bright, fresh flavor. Mint is especially good in savory dishes like (the appropriately named) Chicken with Mint (page 75) or Pumpkin Pork Stew (page 33). Any basic mint at the grocery store works fine for the recipes in this book, though a little goes a long way. Get it to last longer by trimming off the ends and placing in a glass jar like flowers in a vase. Fill the jar with water and then put a plastic bag over the leaves. Tie the bag loosely to protect the leaves and refrigerate. The mint will keep for several days longer than if stored solely in a plastic bag.

Onions and Shallots Yellow and red onions are used throughout the book, with shallots—more common in Myanmar—offered as an alternate. Shallots are kept as an alternative in this book because when many of these recipes were adapted to American kitchens, shallots weren't available at affordable prices. Plus, the European shallots sold in the States are larger than Asian shallots, with a sharper flavor more similar to onions. No matter what you're using, there are a few things to keep in mind. When slicing onions, halve them through the root end and then slice lengthwise into strips, not crosswise. The same goes for shallots—it's rare to see them sliced crosswise into rings. When using either onions or shallots raw, cut out some of the bite by giving them a five-minute soak in cold water, and then drain well, shaking off the excess water.

Thai Basil Just because it's called Thai basil in the United States doesn't mean it's exclusively used in Thai cooking. It's also called for in Chinese stir-fries. At Burma Superstar, it's used when a fresh licorice flavor is desired to brighten up a dish. Look for basil with purple stems and dark green leaves that are skinnier than those of Italian basil. If it's unavailable, skip it or use cilantro instead.

DRIED AND FRESH CHILES

There's a lot of flexibility in what you use, chile-wise, to make the recipes in this book. While Burmese food is not as spicy as Thai, there are plenty of ways to amp up the heat. (And if heat isn't your thing, it's easy to dial it back too.) The heat level of both dried and fresh chiles varies significantly. For dried chiles, chile flakes will be milder than small dried chiles.

On the fresh side, while Thai chiles have a reputation for being the spiciest, sometimes they can be milder than serranos. Jalapeños are generally mild, but now and again one can sneak up on you. If you are unsure about the heat level and are game for an experiment, touch a tiny bit of chile to your tongue. If your tongue starts to tingle immediately, you're probably dealing with a chile that carries some heat. Proceed with caution by removing the seeds and white membrane before chopping the chiles. (And avoid touching your eyes after chopping chiles—ouch!) If the fresh chiles are disappointing in the heat department, pair them with a small dried chile or two to get the spice level you want.

Dried Chile Flakes Readily available dried chile flakes (also called crushed red pepper flakes) give a bit of heat when you bite into a dish. They also can be crushed and infused into oil (see page 221).

Small Dried Chiles There are two kinds of dried chiles you can use for the recipes in this book: chile de arbol and the type of thin-skinned dried Chinese chiles sold by the bag at Asian grocery stores. These Chinese chiles tend to be labeled something along the lines of "dried red chilies," and they are extremely affordable. Both will work for this book. So will any hot dried red chile about 3 inches long (give or take). Breaking one of the chiles in half and adding it to a curry or stir-fry is guaranteed to kick up the heat level nicely. To reduce the heat, shake out the seeds before adding the chiles.

Jalapeños, Thai Chiles, and Serranos Burma Superstar has historically used jalapeños for fresh chiles in salads and stir-fries because their heat level tends to be milder and their grassy chile flavor works well in salads. But at home, the cooks at the restaurant prefer using hotter tiny green or red Thai chiles, buying prepacked bags of them from the produce section at Asian grocery stores. In this cookbook, use either, or opt for serranos, which can add more fire power than jalapeños and are easy to find. No matter which kind of chile you're using, look for smooth, firm peppers with glossy skin.

The influence of both China and India is clear when you take a look at the Burmese spice pantry. From black mustard seeds and cumin seeds to five-spice powder, this collection of seasonings allows for a lot of flexibility. Most of it is widely available too.

Bay Leaves Look for the dried, dusty green–colored bay leaves that you can buy in bulk at Indian, Southeast Asian, or Mexican grocery stores. They have a much lighter aroma and flavor than the forest-green bay leaves from Mediterranean or California bay laurel trees. If you only have fresh bay laurel leaves, use half a leaf or omit; they can be overpowering.

Cayenne and Paprika Both paprika and cayenne are made from ground chiles. Used together, they mimic the heat levels of the kind of ground chile powder favored in Myanmar (which tends to be hotter than paprika but milder than cayenne). At the restaurants, cooks favor paprika for its color and claim it's best when added earlier in the cooking process. Taste before using it, as some paprika batches have nearly no heat and some have a lot. (And avoid smoked Spanish paprika, which has a distinctly different flavor profile than other kinds of paprika.) Cayenne always delivers heat, and it can be added at any point of the cooking process. For the best price, look for paprika and cayenne in the spice section at Asian grocery stores. Instead of cayenne, you can also buy a bag of "hot chili powder" at Indian markets, which essentially provides the same effect as cayenne. For these recipes, avoid American-style chili powder, a mix of cayenne, cumin, and other spices.

Five-Spice Powder Made up of Sichuan peppercorns, cinnamon (or cassia bark), cloves, fennel, and star anise, this spice blend is used only once in this book—for Shan Noodles (page 100)—but it can also be mixed into Pickled Mustard Greens (page 223)

PANTRY SNAPSHOT

Aromatics and Herbs

- Cilantro
- Garlic
- Ginger and Galangal
- Green Onions/Scallions
- Lemongrass
- Mint
- Onions and Shallots
- Thai Basil

Dried and Fresh Chiles

- Dried Chile Flakes
- Small Dried Chiles
- Jalapeños, Thai Chiles, and Serranos

Spices, Dried Herbs, and Seasonings

- Bay Leaves
- Cayenne and Paprika
- Five-Spice Powder
- Garam Masala
- Madras Curry Powder
- Whole Spices
- Palm Sugar
- Salt
- Turmeric

Flours, Starches, and Crunchy Bits

- All-Purpose Flour
- Chickpea Flour
- Cornstarch and Potato Starch
- Rice Flour/Rice Powder
- Suji/Sooji/Farina
- Peanuts
- Sesame Seeds
- Sunflower Seeds
- Yellow Split Peas

Cooking Oils

- Canola Oil
- Coconut Oil
- Peanut and Sesame Oils

Sauces, Dried Shrimp, Pastes, Condiments, and Canned Ingredients

- Canned Coconut Milk
- Distilled White Vinegar and Rice Vinegar
- Fish Sauce
- Oyster Sauce
- Dried Shrimp and Dried Shrimp Powder
- Shrimp Paste
- Rice Wine, such as Shaoxing
- Sambal Oelek and Sriracha
- Soy Sauce, light and dark
- Tamarind Pulp

From the Refrigerator

- Tofu
- Wonton Wrappers
- Spring Roll Wrappers
- Laphet (fermented tea leaves)

for a richer flavor. A pinch of five-spice is also great in a meat or lamb stir-fry. If you don't plan to use it often, buy a small packet (Spicely makes one).

Garam Masala (see page 216)

Madras Curry Powder Sold in packets at Asian markets, Madras curry powder is closer to the curry powder used in Myanmar than Western spice company curry powder blends. It's also less expensive than the glass jars of curry powder sold at American grocery stores. You can choose from Malaysian, Thai, and Vietnamese renditions, and all are generally good. They typically include a blend of turmeric, coriander, cumin, cinnamon, bay leaves, cloves, chiles, allspice, fenugreek, and black pepper. Some are slightly salty. Buy a couple of them to taste and decide which you prefer.

Turmeric Derived from the root of a tropical plant related to ginger, turmeric is one of those wonder spices that fights inflammation and bacterial infections. Fortunately, it also adds a delicate fragrance and flavor to food—it's rare to find a Burmese dish without at least a little turmeric, especially when the dish calls for paprika. It's also typically used in marinades for fish and meat. With this spice, a little goes a long way, and it's okay to scale back on quantity if you're not a big fan of the flavor. (The vibrant yellow-orange powder can stain the tips of your fingers yellow, but the color fades within a day.)

Whole Spices Head to a Chinese or Indian market where you can buy spices in plastic bags at good prices. Because turnover is high, these products tend to be fresher too. Alternatively, some stores sell spices near the bulk bins, which is another convenient way to load up without breaking the bank. Using a coffee grinder reserved for grinding spices is the easiest way to take whole spices to powder form, but an old-school mortar and pestle

gets the job done too. The main spices to buy this way include cumin seeds, green cardamom pods, cinnamon sticks, cloves, and black mustard seeds. If a whole bag of cumin or black mustard seeds is too much for you to use, split it with a friend.

Palm Sugar When traveling around Bagan, a standard-issue tourist stop is to pull over to watch women boil up palm sugar candy in large woks over an open flame. Made from boiling down the sap of the sugar palm, palm sugar (sometimes called *jaggery*) is used all over Southeast Asia and Latin America and comes in countless shapes and colors. For this book, the easiest to cook with is the lighter-colored Thai palm sugar, which comes in 2- to 3-inch rounds that weigh around 2 ounces each. White sugar or unbleached cane sugar can be used in place of palm sugar, though it lacks palm sugar's mild-yet-noticeable caramel flavor.

Salt No need to get fancy here: table salt, kosher salt, sea salt—take your pick. Generally, using sea salt makes dishes a little saltier than using kosher, but when the salt is combined with fish sauce and shrimp paste, the difference is negligible. In Myanmar, food is often seasoned to a saltier level than it is in America (one of the reasons is because MSG use is prevalent; see sidebar, page 237). If something isn't tasting distinctive enough, however, you just might need another pinch of salt. Don't hesitate.

FLOURS, STARCHES, AND CRUNCHY BITS
Split peas, chickpeas, sesame seeds, and peanuts are common crops in the plains south of Mandalay—the central "dry zone." The commodity crops are blended into oils, ground into flour, or fried and eaten as is. In this book, chickpea flour adds body to noodles and salads and helps thicken soups while split peas, sesame seeds, and peanuts boost texture, making salads more dynamic.

Chickpea Flour Light yellow in color, chickpea flour is simply ground chickpeas. It can also go by the name of garbanzo bean flour or *besan*. In flour form, chickpeas add a little heft to salads. Since the flour is naturally gluten-free, it has become much easier to find in non-Asian stores. Look for it in the bulk bins at natural foods stores or with the alternative flours in the baking aisle. Bob's Red Mill makes it. If shopping at an Indian grocery store or Southeast Asian market, look for bags labeled be-san. See page 215 for instructions on how to toast it.

Cornstarch For the Chinese-style stir-fry dishes in this book, starch is a crucial component that helps coat protein and thicken sauces. While this book uses cornstarch for stir-fries, potato starch works just fine in stir-fries, and some prefer it. Cornstarch is also an important ingredient in the Fried Yellow Bean Tofu (page 187), where it helps bind the tofu together. For whatever reason, Kingsford's seems to work better than other brands.

Rice Flour/Rice Powder There are a couple of kinds of rice flour (also called rice powder): regular and the kind made from glutinous (sticky) rice. For this book, regular white rice flour will be all you need. Save the sticky rice flour for making mochi.

Suji/Sooji/Farina This is the main ingredient in semolina cake, one of the most prevalent sweets in Myanmar. The wheat-based flour is easy enough to find at Indian grocery stores but can be tough to locate elsewhere. Grainy in texture, with a pale cream color, it gives the cake its signature soft, chewy quality. The kind of semolina used to make pasta is not a substitute. Instead of *suji*, farina (the main ingredient in Cream of Wheat) can be used. It yields a slightly darker semolina cake, but the texture and flavor are similar. Look for farina among Middle Eastern ingredients at grocery stores. If using farina, make sure it's not a quick-cooking variety with a lot of extra ingredients.

Peanuts The peanuts you see in Myanmar tend to be small, nubby things with the skins partially attached. Burma Superstar buys larger, skinned, and dry-roasted peanuts seasoned with salt, which are easy to find in most U.S. grocery stores. Some peanuts are seasoned with more salt than others. If looking to control the salt level of a dish, buy unsalted peanuts.

Sesame Seeds Sesame seeds are a commodity crop in Myanmar, where they're toasted and eaten in salads or pressed into oil. For the recipes in this book, buy sesame seeds in small batches and store them in the freezer. Sesame seeds go rancid quickly, and nothing takes the thrill out of a meal like crunching into rancid bits of sesame.

To toast a small amount of sesame seeds, heat a dry skillet or cast-iron pan over medium heat. Add 2 tablespoons or so of seeds and toast, shaking the pan often as they pop and toast, until they are aromatic and lightly golden brown, about 2 minutes. If you've toasted more than you need for a recipe, store the remaining sesame seeds in the freezer.

To toast a larger amount of sesame seeds, preheat the oven to 350°F. Put ½ cup sesame seeds on a rimmed baking sheet and bake until golden brown and aromatic, about 15 minutes.

Sunflower Seeds During the monsoon months of June through August, fields of sunflowers are visible along the drive from Bagan to Mt. Popa—home of the indigenous *nat* spirits and a bunch of unruly monkeys. And just east of Mandalay in the hills, the city of Pyin Oo Lwin (a former British hill town called Maymyo) is a major producer of fried sunflower seeds. The great thing about using sunflower seeds to add crunch to Burmese salads is that they're ready to go out of the bag. Look for toasted and shelled sunflower seeds and store extra in the freezer to prevent them from going rancid.

Yellow Split Peas These split peas look a lot like chickpea *dal*—but they're a pea, not a lentil, and have a slightly flatter contour. At Burma Superstar, these dried peas are workhorses. They're fried for salad toppings and mixed into batter for crackers. They're also blended with chickpea flour to make Fried Yellow Bean Tofu (page 187). Before using them, soak them overnight with a pinch of baking soft to soften them.

COOKING OILS

One thing that takes getting used to for the uninitiated is the quantity of oil used in Burmese cooking, especially curries. Traditionally, aromatics would be cooked until the water was cooked out of them and the oil "returned," meaning that it rose to the top of the surface. Nowadays, modern cooks will sometimes start with a solid glug of oil and later ladle half of it out for lighter dishes. Or they use less altogether. Point is, though, that oil is essential to Burmese cooking.

Canola Oil In this book, basic canola oil is the workhorse oil, especially for infused oils, like Chile Oil (page 221), or Garlic Oil (page 211) and Onion Oil (page 208). Use it for deep-frying too. Oil tends to go rancid, so it's better not to use the same oil for frying over and over again. When it has darkened substantially, it's time for fresh oil. Keep an empty plastic bottle handy in which to pour excess oil for easy disposal.

Coconut Oil It's amazing how popular this ingredient has become in a matter of a few years. And it's easy to see why: coconut oil smells (and tastes) amazing. Unlike in South India, however, coconut oil is rarely used in Myanmar. In this book, it is needed specifically to enhance the natural coconut flavor in coconut rice. For best results, get cold-pressed ("virgin") coconut oil, which is much more aromatic.

Peanut and Sesame Oils Peanuts and sesame seeds grow throughout the relatively dry farming areas of Upper Myanmar, near Mandalay, and have long been pressed into cooking oils. When buying these oils, read labels carefully. Neutral peanut and sesame oils—they tend to read "for high heat" on the label—can be used in place of canola oil for the recipes in this book. Like canola, these oils aren't intended to impart flavor, though some peanut oils do have a bit of a peanut aroma. Aromatic unrefined peanut oil can be used like extra-virgin olive oil, drizzled over a salad right before serving and imparting a delicate peanut aroma. This style of peanut oil is especially good in the Namhsan Salad (page 140) and Semolina Cake (page 197).

SAUCES, DRIED SHRIMP, PASTES, CONDIMENTS, AND CANNED INGREDIENTS

Having the following ingredients on hand lowers the barrier for cooking not only Burmese food but also dishes from all over Asia. The good news is they keep for months.

Canned Coconut Milk The crazy popularity for everything coconut has increased the variety and quality of the canned coconut milk available at the grocery store. While it used to be hard to find brands without emulsifiers like guar gum or preservatives, now it's relatively easy to do so. Read the label. When possible, opt for coconut milk that lists coconut as the only ingredient. This often means that the coconut cream will have separated from the milk when you open the can. That's perfectly fine—just give it a stir before measuring, if necessary. Try to only open what you can use. An open can of coconut milk keeps for only a couple of days in the refrigerator, so freeze any extra for longer storage. Avoid anything labeled "lite coconut milk" or "sweetened coconut cream"—that's the stuff for piña coladas, not curry.

Fish Sauce Made by salting small fish (like anchovies), letting them age for months, and then collecting the liquid extracted from the process, fish sauce is an incredible condiment that can be used directly in a sauce or cooked into soups and curries. Not all fish sauces are created equal, so read the label to keep an eye out for additives. One of the best widely available fish sauces on the market is Red Boat. A less expensive alternative is the Three Crabs brand, which has a reliable flavor and clear color. (Avoid murky bottles with sediment.) The quantities of fish sauce given in this cookbook are often provided as a starting point, and some fish sauces are less salty than others. Feel free to add a glug more to up the umami impact or scale back if risk-averse.

Oyster Sauce A popular Chinese kitchen condiment, oyster sauce adds a surprisingly subtle layer of flavor to stir-fries. Made with oyster extract, seasonings, sugar, and starches for thickness, this dark, slightly thick sauce is used in only one recipe in this book (see Fiery Tofu, page 73), but like other Asian sauces, it keeps for months and months in the refrigerator. A spoonful can easily dress up stir-fried vegetables, especially cauliflower or water spinach.

Dried Shrimp and Dried Shrimp Powder When added to salads and noodles, dried shrimp give food an umami layer in a subtler way than fish sauce or shrimp paste. When buying dried shrimp, seek out cellophane packets of pinkish-red shrimp running under an inch long. You can even find Gulf-caught shrimp if you're avoiding imported specimens. The refrigerated sections of Asian markets are usually stocked with packets.

To make dried shrimp powder, in two batches, grind ½ cup dried shrimp in a coffee grinder reserved for grinding spices. If using over the course of a few days, keep out at room temperature or in the refrigerator. If you are going to be using

dried shrimp a lot while cooking through this book, however, grind 4 ounces at a time (which is generally a whole bag) in a food processor. It might take a few minutes to grind the shrimp if they are very cold or frozen. Once ground, the shrimp can be stored in an airtight container in the freezer for up to 6 months.

Shrimp Paste It's pretty much understood that Burmese cooks will always add more shrimp paste to a recipe than what's called for. It took Desmond years to believe that non-Asian customers were willing to eat food cooked with shrimp paste. While pungent and slightly sour smelling, shrimp paste does wonders for adding a complex, savory layer to everything from soup to rice salad. Shrimp paste varies significantly across Southeast Asia. For the recipes in this book, seek out one that is soft enough to scoop up with a spoon (avoid the dried pastes sold in blocks). One of the most flavorful shrimp pastes comes from Shan Shwe Taung, a company based in Mandalay that specializes in fermented tea leaves. If you ever find yourself in Mandalay, visit their slick shop Shan Shwe Taung Tea and Fried Beans #2. Their shrimp paste contains a fair bit of Thai chiles, too, adding a nice kick to dishes—but beware: it can make things spicy. A more widely available all-purpose option is Lee Kum Kee's "Shrimp Sauce," which is smooth in texture.

MSG

In Myanmar, the use of MSG (monosodium glutamate) is pervasive, so much so that Burmese cooks, whether they are working in restaurants or at home, don't think twice of finishing a dish with a pinch or two of the flavor enhancer made famous by Ajinomoto, a Japanese chemical and food conglomerate. While glutamate proteins—the source for umami flavor—are naturally found in foods like tomatoes, seaweed, and Parmesan cheese, MSG is glutamate in salt form.

While many believe "Chinese Restaurant Syndrome" (the after-effects of consuming too much MSG) is a real thing, scientific studies have failed to prove beyond a reasonable doubt that MSG is the source of the headaches, flushing, or other discomforts associated with this alleged syndrome. Still, many see the seasoning agent as a crutch, an easy way to make cheap food taste better. Of course, MSG hasn't been around forever, and many other

ways to enhance the flavor have evolved over the years. With curries and sauces, umami comes from layering flavors—ensuring that the onions are cooked well before the garlic is added. Adding savory ingredients, like dried shrimp, also helps. Tamarind Salt (page 217) is another way to make your mouth water while also adding bright flavor.

But while we don't call for it in the recipes in this book, we felt it was fair to point out that if you're trying to re-create a dish exactly as you've tried it on travels through Bagan, Mandalay, or Yangon, the missing link is probably MSG. As far as using MSG in this book? Add a pinch or two if you'd like. Or don't. No matter what you decide to do, maybe we can all agree to stop vilifying it.

Sambal Oelek and Sriracha Sambal is a simple blend of red chiles, brown sugar, and salt. Just a little spoonful adds fire to Fiery Tofu (page 73) and Chicken with Mint (page 75). Sriracha is sweeter and smoother in texture than sambal, so it's not quite a substitute. Burma Superstar favors "Shark Brand Sriracha Chili Sauce," but ubiquitous "rooster" sauce will do, too. If you don't have either, do your condiment selection a favor and buy both: the sauces are sold next to each other at grocery stores and both last for months and months in the refrigerator.

Soy Sauce The world of soy sauce is broad, and every country that relies on the condiment has its preferred flavor profiles on this dark, salty sauce made from soybeans and wheat. For the purposes of this book, we keep it simple.

Light Soy Sauce: When a recipe in this book call for "soy sauce," the default is "light" soy sauce. A regular bottle of easy-to-find Kikkoman works fine. So does a Chinese-style bottle, like the light soy sauce from Pearl River Bridge. (Don't confuse this with "lite," low-sodium soy sauce; here "light" indicates color, not salt quantity.) For a gluten-free option, you can experiment with tamari, but be prepared for a different flavor profile.

Dark Soy Sauce: Aged for months and finished with molasses, dark soy sauce is used in this book in small amounts to deepen the color of a stir-fry, such as Sesame Chicken (page 79). Pearl River Bridge makes a good one. Its mushroom-flavored superior dark soy sauce works, too. Dark soy sauce is more savory than Thai black soy sauce or Indonesian sweet soy sauce.

White Vinegar Distilled white vinegar is the easiest to find—and most affordable—vinegar on the market. It's used in small increments in this book, particularly in Chinese-style stir-fries. The trick here is keeping the vinegar neutral and using it solely to lift flavors. If you prefer lower acidity, however, you can use rice vinegar (the unseasoned stuff) or dilute the distilled vinegar with a little water.

Tamarind Pulp Tangy tamarind is primed to be the Next Big Thing when it comes to food trends. It's easy to get hooked. Native to East Africa, tamarind trees grow all over Myanmar, and their fresh, tender leaves make a great salad with crushed peanuts. (If you visit the country, be sure to look for it.) Tamarind pulp, which is what we use in this book, comes from the tan pods with brittle outer shells that grow on the trees. When buying tamarind, skip the pods (which are sold in the produce aisle) and look for blocks of purple-red pulp in plastic wrap. They're sometimes labeled "wet seedless tamarind." They are occasionally found in produce sections near the tamarind pods, but a more reliable place to look is by the bottles of Asian and Near Eastern sauces in a well-stocked grocery store. Even though the blocks say "seedless," some blocks contain more seeds than others. Avoid bottles of tamarind concentrate; it is not the best substitute for pulp. Tightly wrapped, the pulp keeps refrigerated for a year. To use, just lop off a piece. Tamarind Water (page 218) made from the pulp is much more perishable. Once you have made tamarind water, use it within five days or freeze it.

FROM THE REFRIGERATOR

The wealth of ingredients available in the refrigerated sections of Asian grocery stores is vast, including rice and wheat noodles, various kinds of pickled mustard greens, and countless other finds. For this book, the main things to stock up on from the refrigerated section are tofu, wonton wrappers, and spring roll wrappers. Keep an eye out for laphet (fermented tea leaf) too. (And even though it's generally thought of as a room-temperature item, dried shrimp are also now often stored in the refrigerated section of grocery stores.)

Tofu While there are several kinds of tofu products of various textures, one or two kinds will serve you well in this book. For recipes such as Fiery Tofu (page 73) or Restaurant-Style Tofu Kebat (page 82), look for super-firm tofu from brands such as Hodo or Wildwood. This tofu tends to be firm and dry enough that it doesn't need to be drained and pressed before stir-frying. For other recipes, such as the Pumpkin Tofu Stew (page 35) or Rainbow Salad (page 95), firm tofu is preferable. Before cooking firm tofu, slice it up and let it drain on paper towels to allow any excess liquid to drain off while you prepare the other ingredients.

Wonton Wrappers Also called wonton skins, these flour-based wrappers come in 12-ounce packages of 3½-inch squares or rounds in the refrigerated section in Asian specialty stores and well-stocked grocery stores. The purpose of them in this book is to add an extra-crispy texture to salads and noodles (and noodle salads)—they fry up quickly and beautifully. However, if you have spring roll wrappers on hand, slice them up and fry them instead. Or keep your eyes peeled for bags of fried wonton skins and use those on top of noodles and salads instead.

Spring Roll Wrappers In this book, these become wrappers for Samosas (page 188). Look for square "spring roll skins" or "lumpia wrappers" 6 to 8 inches long. They can be found in the refrigerated section of Asian grocery stores and the frozen section of other markets. Every so often, they're stocked next to tortillas. If choosing between two brands, go with one that has thinner paper, which allows the wrappers to fry faster. Leftover trimmings or whole wrappers can be fried up and used in place of wonton wrappers.

Laphet Also called pickled tea, laphet is the main attraction of Burma Superstar's beloved Tea Leaf Salad (page 153). Laphet can be purchased as whole unseasoned leaves, but it's far more likely available as a dark green paste already blended with seasonings or a ready-to-go tea leaf dressing. The trick is knowing which kind you have. Generally, whole-leaf tea will weigh less by volume than tea leaf paste. While researching this book, we came across unseasoned packs of laphet called "pickled young tea leaf" imported from Thailand. The whole curled leaves definitely needed seasoning.

If the label is unclear, how can you tell if the leaves you have are seasoned? Bite into the leaf. If it's really bitter, it needs to be soaked in cold water and then drained. You will need to add more salt when you make the tea leaf dressing than if you were using an already seasoned paste. Follow the prompts when making the dressing for the Tea Leaf Salad (page 153). Sometimes laphet comes with oil and seasonings blended in already. This means it's ready to go out of the jar. Tea leaf dressing made this way is becoming more available (and yes, Burma Superstar now sells it under the brand Burma Love). For more on laphet and its origins, read "Eat Your Tea" on page 143.

Tools and Techniques

At the heart of it, Burmese food is simple home cooking done with a minimum of equipment or fancy techniques. In many kitchens, a charcoal burner, a deep wok that doubles as a pot, a pair of scissors (often used instead of a knife), and a cleaver are all that's needed to cook for a crowd. The use of charcoal in these kitchens gives the food the addictive flavor of outdoor cooking, which is hard to mimic in a modern home kitchen. But the rest adapts easily.

STIR-FRYING

With large woks cradled inside round inserts close to the flame, Burma Superstar's wok stations reach BTU levels that far surpass those of an average kitchen stove. Yet home cooks in Myanmar often rely on little more than a wok set atop a charcoal fire, which doesn't get nearly the same amount of heat. So don't get caught up in BTUs: the stir-fry recipes in this book can be made in a wok or a stainless-steel sauté pan on a home stovetop. A cast-iron pan can also be used in a pinch, but it takes longer to heat up and then retains heat, which can result in overcooking the stir-fry. The key is to have all your ingredients prepped before you start cooking.

DEEP-FRYING

With deep-fat fryers, commercial hoods, and oil-disposal systems in place (used oil goes to a local brewery for biofuel), the Burma Superstar kitchens are designed to withstand the heat and mess of frying. Home kitchens are not so lucky, but with a few precautions in place, it is perfectly do-able to fry at home.

First, here's a plea to get you to buy a wok, if for no other reason than to use it for frying. With sloping sides and even heat, woks are perfectly designed for either shallow-frying onions or deep-frying samosas. One bonus of using a wok for frying is that it enhances the wok's surface, deepening its patinav and ensuring it stays seasoned. A Dutch oven is a second among preferred vessels for frying at home. (Since Dutch ovens do not have sloping sides, you may need more oil.) To use less oil overall, fry foods like samosas and falafel in smaller batches to maintain a constant temperature and prevent ingredients from sticking together.

Before you start, have a rimmed baking sheet lined with paper towels to put fried food on when you take it out of the oil. Next, have chopsticks or a slotted spoon handy to agitate the ingredients when they are in the oil. This will also encourage the ingredients to fry evenly. To get started, heat the oil in a wok over medium heat for a minute or two. To test if the oil is hot enough, dip part of the ingredient to see if bubbles form quickly around it. If so, the oil is ready to go.

In cases when you're frying garlic or onions and you need to save the seasoned oil for recipes, line a heatproof bowl with a strainer ahead of time. When the ingredients are done frying, pour them through the strainer so they immediately stop cooking.

BUYING AND SEASONING A WOK

You do not have to buy a wok to cook Burmese food. However, if you're a big fan of stir-fries and Asian food in general, consider the modest investment. A wok is the best vessel for frying, especially samosas, onions, and yellow split peas. With a little bit of care, it is also easy to use—and the more you use it, the more it will like you back.

Look for a carbon-steel wok with a flat bottom that sits directly on a stovetop without a ring holding it in place. (A wok with a round bottom requires placing a ring on the stove to keep the wok upright.) A 14-inch carbon-steel wok with a metal handle (allowing the wok to be put in the oven) is a good way to go. It will be a dull silver when you buy it new, but it won't stay that color long. You might be sold a lid that goes with the wok, which can come in handy but isn't essential. It's easy enough to improvise with a lid from another pot.

Now it's time to season the wok to build up that naturally nonstick patina. According to the Wok Shop in San Francisco's Chinatown, the easiest way to season a carbon-steel wok is in a hot oven. Here's how:

- Heat the oven to 450°F. Scrub the inside and outside of the wok well with soapy water and then pat it dry. Place it over a burner for 30 seconds or so to dry it completely.

- When the wok is cool enough to handle, rub the interior and exterior of it lightly with vegetable oil.

- Put the wok in the oven upside down and bake for 45 minutes. (If the wok is a traditional Chinese cast-iron variety, bake for only 20 minutes.) As it bakes, the wok changes color from a uniform gray to varying degrees of bronze.

Once it's baked, finish the seasoning process. Slice up half of a yellow onion. Heat a tablespoon or so of vegetable oil in the wok over high heat and add the onion, stirring a bit. Cook until the onion slices have charred. This will further darken the wok.

To clean a wok, use the soft side of a sponge. At home the soft side of a sponge works fine. Give the wok a gentle scrub (a little soap won't hurt it) and then dry it well. To ensure it's dried completely, put it back over heat for a minute. One of the best places to store a wok is in the oven. This helps keep rust at bay. If you do get some rust buildup or gummy oily residue, follow the advice of wok authority Grace Young, who recommends heating the wok until it's hot enough to stir-fry, removing it from the heat, and rubbing a big spoonful of salt and half as much vegetable oil into the sides to remove the rust and residue.

Other Pots and Pans A large Dutch oven or deep 6-quart saucepan or pot can come in handy for cooking vegetables. It won't be quite a stir-fry, but the pot will conduct heat well and the high sides will keep the vegetables in place, saving on stovetop cleanup. These vessels are also great for cooking curries.

A large pot—the kind you'd use for making chicken broth—is handy for making *mohinga* and other soups in this book. A small saucepan is also handy for making some of the condiments. As an alternative to a wok, a 10-inch stainless-steel skillet is reliable pulling together a quick stir-fry.

Spider and Small Slotted Spoon
For frying anything, cooking noodles, or lifting vegetables out of a pot of water, inexpensive spiders sold at Asian grocery stores are invaluable kitchen helpers. A small slotted or perforated spoon, is also good for frying smaller ingredients, like yellow split peas and sliced garlic.

Straight-Sided Bamboo or Wooden Spoon
These are invaluable for stirring soup or curries. They double as wok spatulas for stir-fries, since the dishes in this book don't need those metal wok spatulas that can take extreme heat.

Food Processor or Blender A mortar and pestle is all well and good, but for making yellow split pea tofu or tea leaf dressing, dodge the carpal tunnel and use one of these modern devices. To save time, Burmese home cooks in California often skip mincing garlic and onions by hand and instead give the peeled alliums a spin in a food processor (a small one is ideal for garlic).

Coffee Grinder for Spices An inexpensive coffee grinder is arguably better at grinding spices than grinding coffee beans. It's not a good idea to switch between coffee and spices (unless you like your morning cup with a hint of cumin), so keep one for grinding spices only. To clean the blades from pungent spices (or dried shrimp), grind up a small handful of uncooked white rice.

ACKNOWLEDGMENTS

This book is at least 25 years in the making, and our thanks go out to the community that continues to support Burma Superstar.

To Joycelyn Lee, who has been instrumental in building Burma Superstar into a restaurant that has inspired countless people to learn more about Burmese food. Thank you for putting the "Rainbow" in Rainbow Salad and for so much more.

To my daughter, Mya, the best mohinga taste-tester in the business. May this book help you continue to connect with your heritage.

To Carole Bidnick, my agent, who somehow got me to sit down and think that this book was a possibility. Your patience with me was truly remarkable. (And sorry that it literally took us years to return your call.)

To Ten Speed Press
Jenny Wapner, our editor, who supported our quest to dig into the world of fermented tea and let us dedicate several pages to describing how it is made.

Kara Plikaitis, our fearless designer, who put out a wok fire on set during a photo shoot and spent extra time to ensure that the photography was always in sync with the story.

Thanks are also owed to Rachel Markowitz for thoroughly copy editing the text (and even testing a recipe), Elisabeth Beller for proofreading it, Ken Della Penta for indexing it, Erin Welke, for helping get the word out about Burma Superstar—and Myanmar itself, and Ashley Pierce, Kate Bolen, Lizzie Allen, and everyone else at Ten Speed HQ who supported the book behind the scenes. Thank you.

To Our Book Team
Kate Leahy, my coauthor, who not only knows how hot it gets in Bagan in the off-season but also can now cook like a Burmese lady. Her wok was sacrificed in the fire.

John Lee, our photographer, who not only captured the sense of change in Myanmar today but also, during the course of making this book, fended off monkeys at Mt Popa and spent hours hanging out at our restaurants to capture images of our staff.

Lillian Kang, who not only is a talented food stylist in her own right but also got us all to laugh about that wok fire (after the fact). And props to Ethel Brennan (for props).

To Olga Katsnelson and her team for working with us to promote the book and Burmese food.

To the restaurant staff, past and present, and friends who have supported the restaurant, especially (in alphabetical order) Afoo, Pa Bawi, Jacky Chan, Dewey Chi, Chuck Chin, Soo Chyung, Ma Htay, Kent Li, Har San and Rahima, Ma Sein, Carl Velasco, Lynda Vong, Meida Wang, Karen Wong, Daw Yee, and the entire Wu family. The success of Burma Superstar would also not have been possible if it wasn't for your involvement. Special thanks to Nin Thawng, who came in early to coach us on recipes (especially curries), Osama Asif, who was instrumental in connecting us with Carole and helped launch the project internally while manager of the Oakland restaurant, and Tiyobestia Shibabaw, who also helped coordinate cooking sessions and interviews.

To our Mission Street team, especially Jett Yang, for joining us on our Namhsan adventures equipped with a suitcase filled with MREs in case we got stuck in the middle of nowhere (excellent planning!); Irene Cho, who came on to help promote the book and the fermented tea leaf story with her signature amount of enthusiasm and attention to detail; and Amy Lee, who not only was instrumental in organizing our research trips to Myanmar but who also helped vet ideas during the process of creating this book. (Thank you for ensuring we never missed a flight.) Thanks are also due to Jenny Su for always keeping us on track, Ma Mee Shu for taking such good care of Mya, Ryan Hughes for keeping me organized, and everyone

else who has worked behind the scenes to make Burma Superstar and Burma Love what they are today. (My apologies for all of those meetings.)

To our colleagues in Myanmar who have become friends, especially Nelson Rweel, Myo Win Aung, Khin Ye' Yupar Aye, and Bryan Leung. Thank you for sharing your country with us. And to Sarah Oh, our American friend in Yangon, who shared her side of the historic election with us.

To Andrea Nguyen, for tofu support and for connecting Kate with Karen Coates, and to Karen Coates for sharing her Pa-O beans story and for her detailed reporting from Myanmar's countryside.

To Maggie Hicks at the International Rescue Committee and to Zack Reidman and Deepa Iyer of New Roots for helping us better understand the IRC story and refugee life in the Bay Area.

I would also like to thank Rich Cho, James Pollone, Raymond Quan, Eric Rochin, and Mazen Salfiti for always supporting me and my endeavors.

And finally, to my aunt, Helen Ho, who brought my family to the United States, and to my immediate family: my siblings William, Chris, and Phillippa; my dad, Youn; and my mom, Eileen. Thank you for sacrificing so much to ensure your children would have a brighter future.

BURMA
★
LOVE

INDEX

Published in the United States by Ten Speed Press, an imprint of the
Crown Publishing Group, a division of Penguin Random House LLC, New York.
www.crownpublishing.com
www.tenspeed.com

Ten Speed Press and the Ten Speed Press colophon are registered trademarks
of Penguin Random House LLC.

Library of Congress Cataloging-in-Publication Data
Names: Tan, Desmond, 1966- author. | Leahy, Kate, author. | Lee, John, 1971-
    photographer (expression)
Title: Burma Superstar : addictive recipes from a beloved San Francisco Bay
    area restaurant / by Desmond Tan and Kate Leahy ; photography by John Lee.
Description: First edition. | Berkeley : Ten Speed Press, [2016] | Includes
bibliographical references and index.Identifiers: LCCN 2016025785 (print) | LCCN
2016035630 (ebook)

Subjects: LCSH: Cooking, Burmese. | Burma Superstar (Restaurant) |
LCGFT: Cookbooks.
Classification: LCC TX724.5.B93 T36 2016 (print) | LCC TX724.5.B93 (ebook)
| DDC 641.5959/1—dc23
LC record available at https://lccn.loc.gov/2016025785

Hardcover ISBN: 978-1-60774-950-9
eBook ISBN: 978-1-60774-951-6

Printed in China

Design by Kara Plikaitis
Food styling by Lillian Kang
Prop styling by Ethel Brennan

10 9 8 7 6 5 4 3 2 1

First Edition

KATE LEAHY is a writer and the co-author of the *A16 Food + Wine*, the IACP Cookbook of the Year and recipient of the IACP Julia Child First Book Award; *SPQR*; *The Preservation Kitchen*, which Eater.com ranked as one of the most notable books of the year; and *Cookie Love*, one of NPR's top books of 2015. She lives in San Francisco, CA.

DESMOND TAN is the co-owner of the Burma Superstar family of restaurants, which he has grown into three thriving destinations, with more on the way. He was born in Burma and came to San Francisco when he was eleven years old. In 2014, he launched Burma Love Natural Foods Company, one of the first companies in the United States to import Burmese ingredients—most notably *laphet*, Burma's famous fermented tea leaves. He lives in San Francisco, CA.